The Official Book
of the
BOSTON TERRIER

TS-303

TITLE PAGE: The dapper and dazzling Ch. Bo-K's Strike Up the Band, bred by Bob and Karen Milham, was an FCI World Youth Winner and a Junior World Champion.

© by T.F.H. Publications, Inc.

Distributed in the UNITED STATES to the Pet Trade by T.F.H. Publications, Inc., One T.F.H. Plaza, Neptune City, NJ 07753; on the Internet at www.tfh.com; in CANADA Rolf C. Hagen Inc., 3225 Sartelon St. Laurent-Montreal Quebec H4R 1E8; Pet Trade by H & L Pet Supplies Inc., 27 Kingston Crescent, Kitchener, Ontario N2B 2T6; in ENGLAND by T.F.H. Publications, PO Box 15, Waterlooville PO7 6BQ; in AUSTRALIA AND THE SOUTH PACIFIC by T.F.H. (Australia), Pty. Ltd., Box 149, Brookvale 2100 N.S.W., Australia; in NEW ZEALAND by Brooklands Aquarium Ltd. 5 McGiven Drive, New Plymouth, RD1 New Zealand; in SOUTH AFRICA, Rolf C. Hagen S.A. (PTY.) LTD. P.O. Box 201199, Durban North 4016, South Africa; in Japan by T.F.H. Publications, Japan— Jiro Tsuda, 10-12-3 Ohjidai, Sakura, Chiba 285, Japan. Published by T.F.H. Publications, Inc.

MANUFACTURED IN THE
UNITED STATES OF AMERICA
BY T.F.H. PUBLICATIONS, INC.

The Official Book of the BOSTON TERRIER

Muriel P. Lee

A festive trio from Kap's Bostons, owned by Kent and Jane Peters.

About the Author

Muriel P. Lee has been active in the dog world since 1965 when she purchased her first Old English Sheepdog. After finishing four Old English champions, she decided to find a breed that was less bulky and easier to keep. Having grown up with a Wire Fox Terrier, she found it a natural to look at the Terrier Group and eventually settled upon a Scottish Terrier. Over the years she has shown many a Scot and whelped numerous litters for both herself and for her close friend John Sheehan of Firebrand Kennels.

Muriel was a self-employed business woman in Minneapolis for 22 years, owning a drinking and eating establishment just off the University of Minnesota campus. A graduate of the University of Minnesota with a degree in music, she is an avid gardener, and a proficient needle-worker, having had her pieces exhibited in Minneapolis, Charleston, Dallas and Monaco, in addition to the AKC "Bitches in Stitches" exhibition in 1982.

In 1984 she wrote and published her first book *The Whelping and Rearing of Puppies: A Complete and Practical Guide,* which has been the book of choice by many breeders throughout its numerous printings. In 1993, TFH Publications brought out her book *The Official Book of the Scottish Terrier* and she is currently under contract to them for several other breed-specific books.

She has been a member of the Minneapolis Kennel Club for 30 years and has served as treasurer for 20 years. She is a member of the Lake Minnetonka Kennel Club and a member of the Scottish Terrier Club of America where she has been historian and editor of the STCA yearbooks. She is an AKC licensed judge of Scottish Terriers and has given frequent talks on the whelping of puppies.

Muriel resides in a townhouse with a nine-year old "Morris" cat, and two French Bulldogs, Ch. Bushaway Remy LeFox and Ch. Bushaway Bijou LeFox.

The Official Book of the Scottish Terrier, *published in 1993, endorsed by the Scottish Terrier Club of America, and written by author Muriel P. Lee.*

The Complete Guide to Whelping and Rearing Puppies, *an award-winning title by author Muriel P. Lee.*

"Beastly Affairs," postcard printed in England in 1907.

CONTENTS

Introduction

Vincent Perry, the great all-breed dog show judge, wrote, "No better dog—no greater companion."

Ah, the Boston Terrier! The truly All-American dog—smartly turned out and referred to as "The American Gentleman."

The author has read considerably about other canine breeds and she has never seen so many adjectives to describe a four-footed companion: lively, alert and affectionate; a winning disposition; loving, kind and intelligent; devoted, diplomatic and wise; responsible, quick and classy; graceful, stylish and elegant; and of course, smart, adaptable and companionable. Whew!

This book will give you an overview of the Boston Terrier, from historical facts to grooming and breeding. You will read of the pioneers who spent their time and their money, in addition to the giving of their hearts, to make this a strong, sturdy little fellow who would catch the hearts of Americans. You should know about the temperament (well....what more can be said after the above paragraph?) and the care that will be necessary. If you want to show your dog, or work your dog in obedience, you will find out what will be required of both you and your dog. You will learn about the Boston Terrier Club of America, what function a breed club serves and why you may want to belong to either the national or a regional Boston Terrier club. You will read about breeding your Boston, and hopefully, be given some advice that will help you decide if you really want to breed your dog or if you only want to enjoy it as a family companion. And you will read about what is essential in every breed history—the top-producing dogs, the great winning dogs and the breeders who have made all of this possible throughout the last one-hundred years. And most of all, you will learn what a delight it is to own this marvelous dog and that years of enjoyment will be yours when you give your heart to the Boston Terrier.

Not a toy dog, but surely a doll, the Boston Terrier has no rival as a companion dog.

Showing off his gentlemanly ways, Ch. Zodiac's Special Warrior, owned by Mildred Gentry.

Early Development of the Boston Terrier

Although the foundation dogs behind our present day Boston Terrier came from England, the breed was developed and refined in Boston, Massachusetts, and is considered to be a true American breed. The Boston was made up of crosses between the Bull Terrier, the Bulldog and the White English Terrier. (Additionally, crosses were made to the French Bulldog in the early years.) These breeds had been developed as fighting dogs and the original crosses were probably made for the purpose of having a more game, tougher and quicker fighting dog rather than for the development of a new breed.

The first of these dogs for which there are records was named Hooper's Judge, imported from England in 1865 by Robert C. Hooper. Judge was a cross-bred dog that was mostly bulldog and part terrier, possibly the White Bull Terrier. He had the bulldog traits combined with the quicker actions of the terrier. He was a smaller dog than previously seen, weighing about 30 to 32 pounds. He was well up on leg, dark brindle in color with a blazed face, a white collar and a screw tail. Judge is considered to be the key dog in the pedigrees of the 1890s' Boston Terrier.

Judge was bred to Burnett's Gyp, who was lower stationed than Judge, stocky, with a short, blocky head, and weighed about 20 pounds. From this breeding came Well's Eph, a short, dark brindle dog with irregular white markings on his head and with a short face that gave him a "frog-like expression." All four feet were white and he weighed about 28 pounds.

The Countess of Essex was photographed for the famous **Hutchinson's Popular and Illustrated Dog Encyclopaedia** *with two of her favorite Bostons. She was instrumental in bringing the breed to popularity in England in the 1930s.*

Eph was bred to Tobin's Kate, of unknown background, a golden brindle who was well built and low stationed, with a three-quarters tail. The mating of these two dogs produced Barnard's Tom and his sibling, Atkinson's Toby. (Note that in the 1800s dogs, particularly those used for fighting, were labeled with their owner's last name plus a common call name and when ownership of the dog changed, his name likewise changed. Kennel names, as presently used, were not known.) Both Tom and Toby achieved prominence in the breed but Tom was the better known dog. He was described as a red brindle, weighing 22 pounds, with a white blaze on one side of his head, and a white collar and white feet. He also had a screw tail, which his owner tried to have surgically straightened by his veterinarian. He was considered to be a true representative of the Boston Terrier type. Edward Axtell wrote about Tom, "I shall never forget the first visit I made to Barnard's stable to see him. To my mind he possessed a certain type, style and quality such as I had never seen before but which stamped him as the first real Boston Terrier."

Remem—bered as the Father of the Boston Terrier, J. P. Barnard, whose name is attached to the very first modern-type Boston Terriers.

Tom was bred to Kelly's Nell, who was Tom's daughter. She had a good short blocky head and a three-quarters tail. She was a dark brindle and one side of her head was white and the other was brindle, the prevailing markings of the time.

The breeding of these two dogs produced Barnard's Mike, who was a lighter shade of brindle with white marking and a very short tail. Mike had

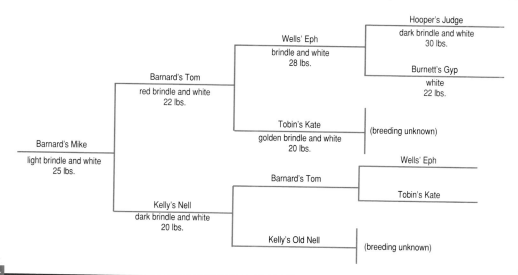

Mrs. William Kuback of Crystal Kennels, in Berlin, Connecticut with Ch. Lady Sensation. The Kubacks were among the breed's honored fanciers in the 1930s.

breeders and their stock.

Charles Kammerer wrote in 1924: "I am going to refer to the original breeders, most of them long since passed to the Great Beyond. But I knew them all, and in my boyhood days it was a treat to go to John Barnard's livery stable on Myrtle Street and see a collection of round heads that you would have hard work to beat today.

"There you would meet such men as Professor Timmy Kelly, owner of Kelly's Nell and breeder of Barnard's Mike. Tim always had a good one, and I have bought a number of good ones from him. Another old timer was Ted Timoney, one of the greatest breeders I have ever known, still alive, aged ninety-two years, and able to take care of himself with any of the boys. Ted was one of the best 125-pound boxers of his time and owned a great many of the earlier dogs.

"Billy O'Brien, who conducted the Club Stable on Chardon Street, was an artist in his line. He owned O'Brien's Ben, one of the earlier stud dogs, and sold to Robert C. Hooper the dog called Hooper's Judge, who was the first ancestor of the true Boston terrier of later years.

"Jim Newman, the florist on Tremont Street, owned many good ones. He was a great admirer of Townsend's Sprig. Frank Barbone, who kept a dog and bird store on Kneeland Street, always had a good one to show you. Pat Donohue, a coachman for a wealthy family on Beacon Street, owned such good ones as Donohue's Bob and Kate, both well known in the earlier days.

full, large, round, expressive eyes—the first to be seen—which he passed on to his progeny with consistency, in addition to passing along his screw tail. By now, the screw tail had became a highly desirable trait and remains a breed characteristic today. He had an even mouth and weighed about 25 pounds.

Barnard's Mike and his sire, Barnard's Tom, were used at stud more than any other dogs of their time. Mike was considered to be the first to portray the twentieth century Boston Terrier and was the sire of Punch, one of the first Boston Terriers registered by the American Kennel Club. Because of these dogs, J. P. Barnard is considered to be the "father of the breed."

As you can tell, colorful names abounded in the early history of the Boston Terrier. One can almost imagine the sights and smells in the streets, alleys, and livery stables of Boston in the late 1800s as you read about the

As presented in Hutchinson's Popular and Illustrated Dog Encyclopaedia, *this is Mrs. G. Mc-Cormick-Goodhart, the first to introduce this American breed into Britain. This is Kandy Kid of Canuck. Many of her dogs went to the kennels of the Countess of Essex.*

"These men used to congregate at John Barnard's kennels on Myrtle Street; and to hear them talk and praise the old round head would make a fancier out of you in short while. Many the day I played hooky from school to go and see a new one at the kennels, or to hear a discussion on the good and bad qualities of the different dogs that were around at the time."

In 1878 Bostons were entered at the New England dog show, held in Boston, in the classes for "Bull Terriers," where they drew a respectable entry. In 1888, Boston provided a class called "Round-headed Bull Terriers, any color," which was judged by John Barnard. Entries were so good that this became a permanent class at the shows. For a period of time, because of this, the Boston Terrier was known as the Round Head or the Boston Round Head.

Dedicated breeders were striving to improve and stabilize their breed, and they showed their dogs in order to get the public acquainted with the breed. While breeding and showing, they also wrote a standard which they felt all dedicated breeders were to follow.

THE EARLY STANDARD

Skull: Large, broad and flat.

Stop: Well defined

Ears: Preferably cut, if left on, should be small and thin, situated as near corners of skull as possible; rose ears preferable.

Eyes: Wide apart, large, round, dark and soft and not "goggle" eyed.

Muzzle: Short, round and deep, without wrinkles. nose should be black and wide.

Mouth: Preferably even, teeth should be covered when mouth is closed.

Neck: Thick, clean and strong.

Body: Deep at chest and well ribbed up, making a short backed, cobby built dog; loins and buttocks strong.

Legs: Straight and well muscled.

Feet: Strong, small and moderately round.

Tail: Short and fine, straight or screw, carried low.

Color: Any color, except black, mouse or liver; brindle and white, brindle or whole white are the colors most preferred.

Coat: Short, fine, bright and hard.

Symmetry: Of a high order.

Disqualifications: Hare lip, docked tail and any artificial means used to deceive the judge.

Weight: It was voted to divide the different weights into three classes, as follows: 15 pounds and under, 25 pounds and under, 36 pounds and under.

Postcard of early Boston Terrier, dated 1906. Courtesy of Sandra Goose-Allen.

POSING FOR HIS PHOTO.

Postcard of Boston Terrier from the collection of Sandra Goose-Allen. Not dated, but likely from early part of the twentieth century.

The present standard recognized by the American Kennel Club has greatly expanded upon and clarified this first standard. Major differences are in the color, ears, and in the mention of markings. The dog has been downsized from 36 pounds to not exceeding 25 pounds in the heaviest weight class.

During the late nineteenth century, the individuals were also working to form a nucleus of breeders who could work together to get approval by the American Kennel Club. In 1889, Charles F. Leland, a prominent breeder, called a meeting that was attended by 40 breeders from around the Boston area. These gentlemen decided to call themselves the American Bull Terrier Club and in 1891, applied for admission to the American Kennel Club Stud Book.

Discussions at Madison Avenue were concerned with two major problems: the name of the breed and the lack of consistency in the breeding programs, caused primarily by crosses to the Bulldog and the Bull Terrier in order to maintain or improve type. In addition, the English Bulldog owners protested that the little dog from Boston would usurp their breed's glory. A committee of three was formed and after some study, each member held a different view on the possibility of admission to the AKC Stud Book. One wrote: "For my own part, I cannot bring myself to favour admitting the dog. I would like to admit the club, but it appears we have to take the dog too."

After two years of discussions between the AKC committee and the Boston breeders, it was determined that only one cross to a Bulldog or a Bull Terrier would be allowed and that could only be in the third generation. In addition, it was decided that since

Dr. Walter G. Kendall, regarded as "the Grand Old Man of the Boston Fancy."

the dog originated in the city of Boston, he should be called the Boston Terrier.

In 1893 the application was resubmitted to the American Kennel Club under the name of the Boston Terrier and on February 27, 1893, the breed was accepted by the AKC as the Boston Terrier and the national club as the Boston Terrier Club of America.

After this, the breed became more standardized and by 1895 the dogs that were being shown were reasonably uniform in type. Markings were more symmetrical and better bodies were built more on the terrier than the bulldog lines. In addition, there was a stabilizing of the gentle disposition. With admission to the Stud Book, the little dog was shown in various sections of the country and it quickly became an American favorite, taking off in unsurpassed popularity and to this day it still remains fairly high on the AKC's list in popularity.

In 1893 there were 75 or so Bostons that were approved for the Stud Book, as they were certified to have been bred pure for at least three generations. These were the dogs that formed the foundation of the Boston Terrier.

At the beginning of the twentieth century, there were several stud dogs that achieved prominence and were used extensively. Yet, William Denlinger wrote the following:

"Even the great stud dogs of the time were seldom good enough to appear high in the awards list and are famous more for their progeny than for their appearance. As sires they were not consistent; two or three champions among perhaps hundreds of sons and daughters made a stud dog notable. It is amazing that such otherwise worthless dogs should have been recognized and bred to as much as they were. Breeding was largely a gamble then, and good results, when they occurred, were credited largely to the sire. Little thought was given to the merits or lack of them in the dam."

Franz J. Heilborn, an early American breeder who produced the famous Raffles.

Particular dogs of note were: Goode's Buster, Sullivan's Punch, Cracksman, Ringmaster and Heilborn's Raffles.

Goode's Buster, grandson of Atkinson's Toby, was a sound but not too attractive dog. He was more of the Bulldog type, with a short neck, low station and sparse markings. On the plus side, he had a nicely shaped head, a well-set-on screw tail and dark "kindly" eyes. A prolific sire, his best known offspring was Ch. Monte. Charles Kammerer wrote that Ch. Monte had the best body, legs, feet and tail he had ever seen in a stud.

Heilborn's Raffles, whelped 1905, a particularly revol–utionary sire from the turn of the century, credited with changing the look of the breed.

Ringmaster (also called Sport IV) was whelped in 1902. He was a rich mahogany brindle with a strong, short head and large, full eyes. He was a prepotent stud who often offset the weaknesses of the females bred to him. He was used extensively at stud because he carried and passed along the type of head that was so desirable at the time, and he founded one of the original lines, or strains, of Bostons.

Heilborn's Raffles, whelped in 1905, was dark in color, (offsetting some of the many golden brindles coming out of Cracksman), small in size and excelled in quality. He sired many champions, but of particular note were his descendants, Ch. Mosholu Blink and Woodward Captain, both of whom, in turn, produced many champions and top-winning dogs. E. J. Rousuck, who wrote *The Boston Terrier* in 1926, dedicated his book to Raffles: "To Heilborn's Raffles, who helped revolutionize the breed from its chaotic mixture of types to its present nearly perfect standardization."

Although there were other dogs that were used for stud, these particular dogs were considered to be the cornerstones of the breed. Probably these early dogs would not have placed in the show ring several decades later but they provided a nucleus for the later breeders to build upon. The breeders were able to improve upon the looks and the disposition of the breed and within short order it became one of the most popular breeds in the country and remained so for many years.

Kipling wrote, "And the woman said, 'His name is not Wild Dog any more, but the First Friend, because he will be our friend for always and always and always.'"

Whelped 1902, Tony Ringmaster with his young master. This dog proved to be an important stud for the breed. He was sired by Ringmaster, bred by M. Glynn and G. J. Kimball of Marblehead, Massachusetts.

Sullivan's Punch, whelped in 1896, had "heaps of type" and was "clean cut as a cameo." He was compact and sound with an excellent eye and expression. He was a predominantly white dog with brindle head markings and produced numerous champions.

Cracksman, whelped in 1898, sired many golden brindles with large, soft eyes. He excelled in expression and had a quieter disposition than had been previously seen. His puppies had great quality but lacked the fire and "zip" that the Punch offspring carried.

Bostons Moving Along in Popularity: 1900

The Boston Terrier truly moved at a rapid pace in the years from 1910 through 1930. The American Kennel Club registered 90,000 Boston Terriers between 1921 and 1934 and from 1905 to 1935 the breed was always in first or second place in the popularity of all AKC dogs. The little breed that had its beginnings in Boston was now well known from one side of America to the other. E. J. Rousuck wrote: "By the early 1900s the little dog was shown throughout the county but it was still known that the best dogs were in Boston. Prices soared! $100 to $150 for a puppy from high-class stock. $100 for a stud service from Ch. Hagerty King!"

Although large numbers of dogs were being bred by many breeders and many litters were being produced, only a few dogs from the numbers being produced would end up making an impact upon the breed. These specific dogs became notable principally through the quality of their offspring, the prepotency of the stud, and on occasion the popularity of an animal either because of his show wins or because of the publicity by his owners.

In general, credit is given to the following six dogs that became cornerstones of the breed. These six dogs represented three strains that were carried in pedigrees in the breed for decades and if one were to follow a pedigree back far enough on your present dog (if you could find a piece of paper big enough to get all of those generations in!) one, or more, of these studs would be in everyone's pedigree. The six dogs were: Ch. Hagerty King, Ch. Mosholu Blink, Sigourney King, Woodward Captain, Intruder and Ch. Prince Conde.

The ideal medium between terrier and bulldog, Ch. Hagerty King was whelped in 1916 and bred by Mrs. Dan Hagerty and purchased by Mrs. George Dresser.

Ch. Hagerty King, whelped in 1916, was a 14-pound dog who was considered to be a happy medium between the terrier and the bully-type Boston. He excelled in head and muzzle and some felt that he was the most perfect specimen ever produced—or at least that had been produced up to that time. King (and some called him "Faultless King") was bred by Mrs. Dan Hagerty and purchased for $2500 (a large sum of money in those days!) by Mrs. George Dresser. He was a cross between the Ringmaster and Raffles

A popular stud of his time bred by A. A. Appel of Philadelphia and later owned by Mrs. Edward G. Graves of Detroit, Ch. Prince Conde is regarded by historians as a pillar of the breed "ahead of his time." He sired eight champions, including BIS winners.

strains. He was a black and white dog with a touch of tan. Black and black and tan were considered disqualifications in those days, but he still made up his championship based upon his superior type, in addition to being Winners Dog at Westminster in 1918. He was not used at public stud and sired five champions from the few bitches that were bred to him.

Intruder, whelped in 1915, was the most promoted dog in Boston Terrier history up to that time. He was bred to many bitches and there was little uniformity among his offspring. He was retired from public stud in 1926 and it was rumored that he earned over $2500 for his owner. An advertisement read, "What Babe Ruth is to Baseball, so Intruder is to the Boston Terrier. $4000 turned down for Intruder...I will breed one female each month to Intruder, balance of time will be devoted to picked up brood types at $175." Intruder was down from the Ringmaster strain. Again, although he produced only four champions, his influence upon the breed was great—disputed whether for the better or for the worse—because he had been used so widely. His name appeared in many pedigrees and later appeared in the background of some famous winners. George Schrammel, life member of the Boston Terrier Club of America, wrote in the July 1976 *Boston Bulletin,* "Intruder as a specimen was not truly of the 'Terrier' type but more or less was what some breeders would refer to as being of the 'Bullie' side due to his robustness but which, at the same time, contributed immensely to his dynamic personality."

Woodward Captain was said to have had the ideal head with lovely dark eyes and an expression that Vincent Perry called, "God-love-it." He was a combination of the Raffles, Derby and Ringmaster strains and sired ten champions. He was owned by Frank Caelato of New York City.

Ch. Mosholu Blink was whelped in 1917. He was a seventeen pound golden brindle with ideal conformation and he passed these qualities on to his offspring. He was said to be a "scrapper and a gentleman," tracing his lineage back to the Raffles strain. He had the ability to pass his marvelous traits on to his descendants in the second and third generations. He produced ten champions and was awarded the challenge cup at Westminster in 1924, 1925 and 1926 for "Best Non-Sporting Dog and One of His Get". He passed on to his offspring clean heads, free from wrinkling, an alert expression and his great spirit. The champions he sired were superior to himself. Vincent Perry wrote, "He was all dog in every way—sound as they make them. He lorded it over kennel and ring." He was owned by Mrs. M. C. McGlone of New York City, whose kennel contained up to 90 dogs at times and she raised and owned more than 30 champions. Blink's best known offspring was Ch. Little Tommy Tucker II.

Ch. Little Tommy Tucker II, sired by the famous Ch. Mosholu Blink.

Sigourney King, whelped in the mid-1920s, had four crosses to Raffles and was considered to be the best linebred male of his day. He was a prolific sire and his advertisements called him, "The Peter the Great of Boston Terriers." He once was entered at a specialty show in the stud dog class with 26 of his get!

Ch. Prince Conde was a dog who was almost ahead of his time, appearing "frail" compared to other dogs of the day. He was a 16 pounder, refined, and streamlined with a good front. He sired eight champions, including several Best in Show offspring. William Denlinger referred to him as "apparently a good individual."

The Boston continued to gain in popularity as the century moved along. It was noted that after 1920 the breed became so popular that Boston Terriers could make up twenty percent or more of the entry at an all-breed show and that at specialty shows it could have as many as 200 entries. (Remember that

Whelped 1917, Ch. Mosholu Blink, owned by Mrs. M. C. McGlone of New York City.

these numbers are inverted now—all-breed shows in the 1920s had an entry of 400 to 600 dogs compared to present-day shows of entries up to 3500; specialty shows, except for the National Specialty, may have entries of only 45 or 50 now.) Between 1920 and the 1960s, the Boston Terrier ranked continuously in the top ten breeds of popularity, and during many of those years it was ranked either number-one or number-two.

Boston Terrier kennels were appearing across the country, producing winning dogs in the show ring, bitches who were producing well in the whelping box and stud dogs with many champion offspring. In spite of the transportation problems of the times, puppies in the East were purchased by those in the West, and Western dogs were sent east for dog shows. Trains were the mode of travel for long distances, with dogs traveling in wooden crates through all kinds of weather. Unknown to these pioneers of the breed were airplane travel or the fancy buses that are seen nowadays at dog shows!

In the East, A. Droll and Benny Rosenbloom owned the Hagerty Kennels in New York. Their most famous dog was Ch. Hagerty Again, whelped in 1926, and sire of 16 champions., His great grandsire was the famous Ch. Hagerty King and his sire was Ch. Hagerty King Junior's Son. He was shown sparsely but was Best in Show in 1928 at the New York specialty. Pearl Highby

Ch. Haggerty's King Junior's Son, owned by Droll and Rosenbloom of Brooklyn and Ch. So Big of Sunny Hill, owned by Mrs. E. A. Rine of Caldwell, New York.

Posing with a Boston Terrier on the beach, Joan Crawford on this German postcard from the 1920s.

4906/1

Int. Ch. Rockabye Dempsey, owned by Mrs. Hilda Ridder of New York City. Dempsey and his brother Ch. Rockabye Tunney were whelped, is reported in the August 1930 AKC *Gazette*, on the evening of the famous Jack Dempsey—Gene Tunney championship boxing match.

Goundrey wrote, "He apparently has been kept at home with his nose on the grindstone, earning his bread and butter by producing quality puppies out of different dams." He was a sturdy dog, not built on the terrier lines that were popular at the time, and he helped to bring the breed around again to the desirable medium stationed dog. His most famous offspring was Royal Kid.

Mrs. Hilda Ridder, another New York City breeder, owned the Holiday Kennels. She lived only two blocks from Broadway, close to the Hudson River. The apartment adjacent to her was remodeled as a kennel and the dogs used the backyard garden for exercise. At one show, her dogs won "$56.00 in cash, two cured hams and a gold mesh vanity bag." She purchased Ch. Rockabye Dempsey for $1500 from Dr. Gustav Brandle of Chicago. Dempsey was a 14-pound dog of a rich mahogany color, and it was said that he was one of the greatest light weights up to that time He was an international champion and a popular sire.

Another Boston Terrier breeder from New York City was Alva Rosenberg at Ravenroyd Kennels. He owned Ch. Ravenroyd Rockefeller (out of Ch. Million Dollar King), who sired seven champions. This dog was later sold to E. H. Morse of Flint, Michigan and did much to improve the breed in that part of the country. Vincent Perry wrote that he was a clean, big (25-pound) dog who was appreciated best by those who really knew the breed. He had superior type, a beautiful head and an excellent front. He was the type of dog to be bred to for the improvement of the breed. His best known offspring was Ch. Rockefeller's Ace.

Alva Rosenberg was a highly respected all-breed judge, judging until he was well along in years. He had been charmed by a Boston as an eight-year old boy and remained a fan of the breed all of his life. Anna Katherine Nicholas, who wrote *The Boston Terrier* in 1988, dedicated her book to Alva Rosenberg, as well as

Ch. Rockefeller's Ace, whelped 1932, bred and owned by Mr. and Mrs. Paul Schwartz and later owned by W. C. Ely, Jr.

Ch. Rockefeller's Ace

Ch. Dallen's Spider
Ch. Peters King
Judy P
Ch. Million Dollar Kid
Brownell's Monte Carlo
Shackford's Babe
Peterson's Babe
SIRE: Ch. Ravenroyd Rockefeller
St. Peter's King
Kirtland King
Billie Stutz' Beauty
Beauty King IV
Prince Stutz
Peggy Stutz III
Pretty Mickey VI

Griswald Invader
Ch. Introduce Me
Eastview Cora
Ch. Rockabye Tunney
Woodward Captain
Ch. My Rockabye Baby
Lyons Queenie
DAM: Up For Inspection
Ch. Ace of Aces
Rickenbacker
Sister E
Margies Cinders
St. Botolph's Perfection King
Cedar Hill Tiny
Grants Tiny II

Vincent Perry and Joe Faigel, all three old Boston men and highly regarded dog men.

In Allentown, Pennsylvania., Mrs. E. P. Anders founded the Royal Kennels, where the well-known stud dog Royal Kid, sire of 23 champions, resided. His best known offspring was Ch. Royal Kid Regards, who sired 18 champions, in addition to having had four Bests in Show. He weighed 12 pounds and consistently sired small dogs. The Royal Kid strain produced dogs with strong heads, small eyes and good markings.

Int. Ch. Flash Again, owned by Mrs. H. C. Hayhurst of Illinois, was considered one of the great sires of the day. A 15-pound dog, going back to Ringmaster and Ch. Hagerty King, he sired 11

The oft-quoted dog man, Vincent G. Perry, the famous all-breed judge who helped nurture the Boston Terrier throughout his life. He bred and owned Bostons and proudly acclaimed the breed the most worthy of all.

Ch. Ravenroyd Rockefeller, whelped 1925, sired by Million Dollar Kid, owned by the Cristo Kennels.

champions, of which 6 became international champions. He was a great producer and the foundation base of the Flash Again line. He produced puppies with beautiful balance, strong heads and very dark, full eyes. He was said to have "unusual brain power." Although he produced many puppies, his best ones were the bitches, which were said to all look alike...a true sign of a prepotent stud.

Mrs. W. E. Porter of Denver, Colorado, acquired her first Boston in the early 1900s. Although shows were few and far between in the West at that time, within 25 years she had finished 17 champions under her Kingway Kennel name. Mrs. Porter, along with her friend, Signe A. Carlson, not only bred for the ring but bred for the companion dog as well. They raised winning Bostons for many years and

Ch. Million Dollar Blink, owned by the Cristo Kennels.

eventually took under their wing the young Leonard Myers.

The Million Dollar prefix included two top dogs: Million Dollar Kid, owned by the Cristo Kennels, won the National Specialty show in 1925, and his son, Million Dollar King, of the BaRo Kennels, won in 1926. "Kid" was also the sire of Ch. Ravenroyd Rockefeller. Both dogs won Westminster in 1925 and 1927 respectively. Ch. Million Dollar Kid Boots, grandson of Million Dollar Kid, sired nine champions and was a prominent name in the pedigrees of many of the top winners of the day. Vincent Perry wrote that because he influenced his progeny so favorably his place in the Boston Terrier hall of fame was secure. Kid Boots, owned by Mrs. Jesse Thornton of Baltimore, was a winner at Westminster in 1930 and 1932, as well as winner of the Boston Terrier Club of America specialty shows in 1931, 1933 and 1934.

Am-Can. Ch. Royal Kid Regards sired 18 champions himself and was sired by Royal Kid, owned by Mrs. E. P. Anders.

Ch. Million Dollar Kid Boots, owned by Mrs. Jesse Thornton of Baltimore, Maryland.

Ch. Million Dollar Kid Boots

Suntaug King	Ch. Dallen's Spider
Sigourney King	Ch. Peters King
La Tosca	Judy P
Ringmont Tiny King	Ch. Million Dollar Kid
Rockdale Jr.	Brownwell's Monto Cristo
Weidner's Sunny Girl	Shackford's Babe
Weidner's Callic	Peterson Baby
SIRE: Katinka Going Up	**DAM: Kernwood Rita**
Ch. Arroyo Anarchist	King Toss
Intruder	Ch. Fairlawn Talk O'The Town
Nibbs II	She'll Do
Little Batice	Sallyanna of Naumkeag
Dan Star	McCarthy's Master
Miss Katinka	Suttons Lady of Tangerine
Lady XXXIII	McCarthy's June

Mr. and Mrs. Julius Fangman of Rochelle Park, New Jersey, owned the Monte Carlo Kennels, where they had extensive kennel facilities and where five or six generations of Boston Terriers could be seen by a visitor. A lengthly article in the November 1928 *AKC Gazette* notes that on his visit to the kennel, the writer saw about 35 brood bitches, 5 stud dogs and several dozen puppies. He stated that every Boston he saw looked like a good Boston and that the owners matched and mated their Bostons as carefully as "a jeweler selects his diamonds for a special ring." On occasion there would be up to 20 bitches in whelp at the same time. The Fangmans produced many

extensive facilities, with a staff to care for and show the dogs. With the Great Depression in the 1930s, followed by World War II, dog breeding and exhibiting changed and it came into the domain of the average American who could own only three or four dogs. At the present time, a kennel (of any breed) housing 10 to 20 dogs is considered a large kennel. In addition, the owner is raising the litters, cleaning the pens, and often showing the dogs. With luck, they are able to find a reliable high school student to come in the afternoons and help out. Breeding and showing is now a labor of love.

We will end this era of the Boston Terrier with Vincent Perry of Globe Glowing Kennels. Mr. Perry, considered

An advertisement run for Ch. Million Dollar Kid Boots at stud.

winners and were active in the breed for several decades. Mr. Fangman was also active in French Bulldogs and judged both breeds.

It should be noted that the Boston Terrier, as was true with most other purebred dogs in America, was often championed by the well-to-do who appreciated a beautiful well-bred dog as much as they appreciated well-bred winning horses. Many kennels were owned by the wealthy who could afford

by many to be one of the great dog men of the twentieth century, acquired his first Boston in 1918 and remained active in the breed until his death in 1985 at the age of 87. Born in Canada and a reporter for the *Globe* newspaper in London, Ontario, his best known Bostons were Ch. Globe Glowing All By Himself, sire of 18 champions and Ch. Globe Glowing Perfection, sire of 17 champions. For a time, All By Himself was in the background of the majority of the top-winning dogs in the West. Perfection was sired by Ch. Hough's Ringside Perfection, who was considered to be a top sire, producing puppies with correct markings and the desired tails.

In addition to breeding fine Boston Terriers, Mr. Perry was a well-known writer, an actor and a very popular all-breed judge. He wrote four Boston Terrier books and was a contributor of articles to dog magazines. A winner of many awards in all areas, he was well-

judge dogs of all-breeds and go over hundreds of dogs a year.

The breed dearest to my heart has always been and always will be the Boston. God bless the American dog. He is so beautiful, so devoted and so worthy. If I am permitted a prayer, let it be this: May we of today, and you of tomorrow, be worthy of the Boston Terrier. He is pure, pure gold."

Clearly, the Boston Terrier, with his beginning in the stables of Boston, had within a few generations, reached into the hearts of the rich as well as into Everyman's heart. His size, wonderful disposition and his "gentlemanly" way made him a clear American winner.

E. J. Rousuck wrote in 1926: "The Boston is known and loved by connoisseur and layman. As all classes have participated in his breeding, so have all classes shown a willingness, even an eagerness to buy him. This little aristocrat who has so caught the fancy of his homeland is as distinctly American as a catcher's mitt,

Ch. Globe Glowing Perfection, sire of 17 champions and owned by Vincent G. Perry.

known for his storytelling ability, his wit and his charm. Throughout his life he was a champion of the breed and always appreciated, and could find, a superior specimen

A tribute that Art Huddleston wrote to Vincent Perry in the *Boston Bulletin* included a quote from Mr. Perry: "I

and he has repaid his backers for all the trouble and the work that have gone into his making. He has repaid the debt with interest by a continued heaping up of value for value received. He is now indispensable to the world of dogs, and if handsome is as handsome does, then surely is he the handsomest of them all."

1940s Through the 1960s

Int. Ch. Emperor's Ace, owned by Fred and Mary Lucas of New York, was a Westminster favorite and a multiple BIS winner.

The years during World War II did not seem to affect the Boston Terrier probably because it was such an American breed and the fanciers were not dependent in any degree upon European or English dogs for their breeding stock. The little Boston continued on in popularity and there were breeders throughout the country who were producing high-quality dogs that were winning the highest awards at the most prestigious shows.

Although it is somewhat difficult to place breeders and dogs within a decade or two, I have attempted to place the breeders in the era where their dogs had the most impact, either through their show wins or through the stock they produced.

H.M.S. Kennels of Mrs. Don Smith, was active in the late 1930s and 1940s. Ch. H. M. S. Kiddie Boots, whelped in 1935 and living to the age of 15, was their most notable bitch. Her son, Ch. H.M.S. Kiddie Boots' Son won ten Groups and won the Boston Terrier Club of America national specialties in 1941, 1942 and 1944. He was also three time winner of the Davis Cup, presented by the BTCA in honor of the first president of the national club. He sired numerous champions. H.M.S. Kiddie Boots was out of Ch. Kid Boots Ace and her grandsire was Ch. Million Dollar Kid Boots. All told, winners of a high caliber in all four generations. Vincent Perry wrote that Boots' Son had a

An advertisement for Int. Ch. Emperor's Ace and his sire Ch. Ace's Ace at stud.

head that defied criticism: "His expression, so alive yet so soft and appealing, was lovely."

Fred and Mary Lucas of New York, owned Int. Ch. Emperor's Ace, Best of Breed at Westminster in 1944, first in the Group at that show in 1946 and a winner of several all-breed Bests in Show. When he won the Group at Madison Square Garden, an article from "Memories of the Past" in the *Boston Bulletin,* December 1964 said: "No doubt those at ringside that day cheered until the rafters of old Madison Square Garden shook, because here was a really outstanding specimen of the breed." He was a direct descendant of the Rockefeller strain, being out of Ch. Ace's Ace, whose sire was Ch. Rockefeller Ace. The Lucases also owned Ch. Emperor's Lady DTS who was Best of Breed at Westminster in 1954 and winner of the BTCA National Specialty in 1955.

Charles Cline of California owned Ch. Payson's Miss Patricia G.G. This little gal traveled 35,000 miles a year to dog shows...not an easy feat in the 1940s! She was the winner of 46 Groups

and 19 all-breed Bests in Show. In 1949 she placed second in the Group at Westminster and was the recipient of the Quaker Oats award for the top Boston Terrier of the year. Denlinger wrote, "as a show dog she was full of the old nick and barked at everyone who tried to pet her."

Ch. Payson's Miss Patricia G.G., winner of 107 BOBs and 62 Group firsts, bred by Mrs. Mary Payson and owned by Charles D. Cline, who purchased her for $2500 in 1948 after the NY specialty.

In his day, the top-winning Boston Terrier, Int. Ch. Mighty Sweet Regardless, owned by Mr. and Mrs. Claude Fitzgerald, whelped in the 1940s.

Int. Ch. Mighty Sweet Regardless

Ch. Hagerty Again	Ch. Hagerty Again
Royal Kid	Ch. Bantam Hagerty
Ch. Dixie Romance	Gottlieb's Leading Lady
Ch. Royal Kid Regards	Hagerty's Personality
Personality Again	Ch.RavenroydRockefeller
Horn's Lady Queen	Personality Play Girl
Winnie Mae F	Ch. Sunni Girl
SIRE: Ch. Regardless	**DAM: Fascinating Personality**
Ch. Yankee Boys High Step'r	Ch. I'm The Guy
Ch. Stepper's Gallant Son	Ch. Grand Slam
Gallant Lady Gay	SweetheartofI'mTheGuy
Stepper's Gallant Beauty	Dixie's Hi Hat
Tiny Peters King	Little Ceaser II
Miss Beauty Peters King	Dixiana Black Beauty
Tiny Gal III	Miss Nibs-In

Am-Can. Ch. Mighty Sweet Regardless, whelped in the 1940s, was a very special Boston and the top-winning Boston of all time. Sired by Ch. Regardless and owned by Claude and Bessie Fitzgerald of Wyandotte, Michigan, she began her career at six months of age, taking Winners. Not long after, she was Best of Breed at the Detroit specialty and from then on her career moved rapidly. In New York in February, 1945, she was Best of Breed from the classes at the specialty (entry of 123) and the next day she finished at Westminster in a large entry by going Best of Winners and Best of Opposite Sex to Ch. Emperor's Ace, who went on to win the Group later in the day. Leonard Myers wrote: "She dared judges to put her down; she generated such electricity and excitement in the ring that even her toughest competition both loved and envied her." She was Best in Show at the Chicago International Kennel Club show, winning the Group under Alva Rosenberg and show under Geraldine Rockefeller Dodge, both highly regarded judges. She won the Group at the Westminster show in both 1947 and 1948. Her record is 28 Bests in Show, additional bests in Canada and winner of 13 specialties. Although she was never bred, she made her mark upon the breed by being such an exceptional ambassador for the Boston Terrier.

Leonard Myers wrote an interesting aside about showing during the 1940s: "For a time during her show career, this country was in the grips of gas rationing, making it difficult to attend distant shows. Unless one saved enough coupons for gasoline, the only alternative was to travel by train, and they were very crowded." It's hard for me to believe that anyone younger than 50 years of age even knows what gas coupons were!

Following the deaths of both Mrs. Porter and Miss Signe Carlson, Leonard Myers continued the Kingway prefix for awhile out of love and respect for these two ladies. For a short period of time, he opened his own kennel under the Silver Dollar prefix. Ch. Silver's Fancy Chap was an all-breed Best in Show winner from the bred-by-exhibitor class. Mr. Myers bred numerous champions, Group winners and specialty winners, most of which were shown by himself. He has judged Boston Terriers since the early 1960s and judged the prestigious 100th anniversary show in Boston in 1991. The true mark of one who contributes greatly to a breed is the breeder and owner-handler. Mr. Myers has truly epitomized this individual as one who not only has bred his dogs but has trained and shown them, often taking the top spot of the day. This not only takes knowledge, dedication and money but a tremendous amount of patience and love! In addition, I have to give my sincere thanks to Mr. Myers for reading over the breed history of this manuscript and making corrections and additions as needed.

Indeed, the little Boston Terrier surely has friends who give of their time and talents to look after the breed.

Anne and Bob Griffing were breeders and owners of Ch. Griffing's Little Chappie. They sold this dog at ten months of age to Miss. Signe Carlson from Kingway Kennels. He sired 19 champions, of which 5 were all-breed Best in Show winners, exceptional in any breed. One of his offspring was Ch. Silver's Fancy Chap, also an all-breed Best in Show winner, owned by Leonard Myers. The pedigree for Ch. Silver Sonata, owned and bred by Mr. Myers, reveals a tightly bred dog with the key dog in the pedigree being Ch. Griffing's Little Chappie. Another Best in Show winner, Ch. Chappie's Regards, was owned by John Robinson.

Louise Grant, a breeder of Bostons since the 1930s, owned Ch. Royal Command's Ebony Prince, all-breed Best in Show winner, multiple Group winner, in addition to multiple Best in Specialty Show winner. He was number-one Boston in 1979, sired by Int. Ch. Grant's Royal Command II. Ch. Grant's Royal Command was the sire of 36 champions and winner of the National Specialty in 1956 and again in 1958. For five years

including Ch. Toy Town's Hi Stepping Star Trek, sire of 13 champions, bred by John LoPorto and owned by Elaine Newbecker.

Florence Dancer, owner of the famous Iowana Kennels in Des Moines, Iowa, bred beautiful dogs that were especially noted for their classic heads. Her line is behind many winners. Owning Bostons since 1921, she bred to the best dogs available and she knew good dogs and bred good dogs, producing over 60 champions. She was active in several

Ch. Command's Honey Boy

	Int.Ch.RoyalKid'sSpecialty	Int.Ch.RoyalKid'sSpecialty
Royal Special		Royal Special
	Delaney's Sparkle Plenty	Delaney's Sparkle Plenty
Int. Ch. Grant's Royal Command		Int. Ch. Grant's Royal Command
	Ch. Royal Parader	Ch. Royal Parader
Royal Milady		Royal Milady
	Tootsie XI	Tootsie XI
SIRE: Ch. Grant's Royal Command		**DAM: Ch. Command's Bit O'Honey**
	Ch.Iowana'sFancyBoots	Int. Ch. Grant's Royal Command
Ch. Iowana's Black Velvet		Ch. Grant's Command
	Ch. Aces Cover Girl	MadonnaO'RhyhmsRegard
Velvet Lady of Bar None		Command's Midge
	Master Tee of Bar None	Escort's Gallent Son
Mister of Bar None		Gallant Son's Mitzie
	Wolff's Royalty Mamie	Grant's Madonna

running, he was the sire of either the Winners Dog or Winners Bitch at Westminster. Ch. Grants Royal Command II was the sire of 24 champions and was top Boston Terrier sire for 1969 and 1971. He was noted for his head, type and temperament. Mrs. Grant was also a fine judge of Boston Terriers.

Marie Ferguson, breeder, professional handler and judge (at that time, professional handlers could judge) from Chicago, not only bred many good dogs but showed other dogs to top wins for their owners. Ch. Tops Again's Duke of Regards produced 21 champions,

breed clubs, a staunch breed supporter and a respected judge of the Boston. She bred and owned two all-breed Best in Show winners, Ch. Iowana's Velvet Coquette and Ch. Iowana's Fancy Flair. She had excellent bitches that she bred to the leading sires, and her puppies were in high demand. A nicely bred bitch with Ch. Iowana's Fancy Boots key in her pedigree, Fancy Flair was owned by Mrs. Henry Dunham. She was the winner of 222 Bests of Breed, numerous Group placements and all-breed Bests in Show.

Dr. K. Eileen Hite was very active in the East. Her kennel included Ch.

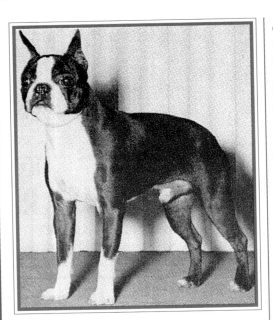

Ch. Royalty's Iowana Jetaway, owned by Craig and Marie Ferguson.

Chappie's Little Stardust, sire of 19 champions and his offspring included his first champions, Ch. Star Q's Brass Buttons and Ch. Star Q's Pease Knutu. Ch. Chappie's Little Stardust won the National Specialty show in 1966 and his son Brass Buttons, a 13-pound dog, won the specialty show in 1969 and 1970. In 1971, yet another son, Ch. Star Q's Pease Knutu won the national. Buttons has four all-breed Bests in Show and was the winner of the Group at Westminster in 1970. In addition, he was the sire of two Best in Show dogs. It was said that he had "a little button of a nose and a button of a tail." Ch. Star Q's Pease Knutu, known for his style and personality, won eight all-breed Bests in Show and had 53 Group firsts as well as 187 Group placements. He was a Group winner at Westminster and number-one Boston in 1972, 1973 and 1974 and was the number-six Non-Sporting dog in 1973.

Harry Clasen's interest in the breed as an owner, breeder and handler, covered nearly six decades, from 1906 until his death in 1975. He had an eye for the breed and a talent for knowing and recognizing quality. He was a former president of the BTCA and a judge of Bostons. He showed Dr. Hite's dogs, Ch. Star Q's Brass Buttons and Ch. Star Q's Pease Knutu. In 1970 he handled the Buttons dog to Group first at Westminster. He owned Am-Can. Ch. Mr. Fancy Boots, sired by Ch. Iowana's Fancy Boots Ace. Fancy Boots had many wins and sired numerous champions. Mr. Clasen bred Ch. Clasen's Cover Girl to Boots, which produced high-quality puppies. In 1964, *Popular Dogs* magazine chose Cover Girl as "the kind you like to judge, the near perfect Boston." His Ch. Toby Junior II won many Groups and was a top ten Boston in 1973 and 1974. Ch. Clasen's Bit O'Honey was third in the Group at Westminster and Int. Ch. Clasen's Mel-O-Nee Maid, owned by Bert Allen, was Best of Breed at the National Specialty in 1950. In addition to the Boston Terrier, Mr. Clasen also exhibited pigeons and was interested in hunting and jumping horses. Indeed, a versatile man!

Anna Katherine Nicholas wrote, "Harry Clasen used to say that it took him ten years of showing before he got his first purple ribbon, which is typical of the earlier days in the fancy when we made haste more slowly than in our modern world. This is probably why our veteran dog men have so thorough a knowledge as they have, as more time then went into learning one's breed thoroughly from basics on forward." When I wrote the book on the Scottish Terrier, one of the great Scottie breeders wrote that it took 15 years of showing before she got a blue ribbon. She learned her trade, though, and had the top-winning Scottie in the country in 1959 and 1960. Too often we are so anxious to reach the top

Am-Can-Mex. Ch. Iowana's Fancy Flair, owned by Henry W. and Loretta Dunham.

Ch. Iowana's Fancy Flair

Ch. Royal Kids Specialty
Royal Special
Delaneys Sparkle Plenty
Int. Ch. Grant's Royal Command
Royal Parader
Royal Milady
Tootsie XI
SIRE: Iowana's Royalty Command
Ch. Iowana's Fancy Boy
Ch. Iowana's Fancy Boots
Ch.TimmiesSunshineCandy
Iowana's Liza Boots
Int.Ch.DeMents'HandsomeCrusader
Miss Fortune
Ch. Aces Cover Girl

Ch. Iowana's Fancy Boy
Ch. Iowana's Fancy Boots
Ch. Timmies Sunshine Candy
Iowana's Fancy Boots Model
Ch. Iowana's Velvet Gigelo
Iowana's Velvet Gigelette
Iowana's Ocette Sugar
DAM: Miss Penny Boots Gidget
Ch. Iowana's Fancy Boy
Ch. Iowana's Fancy Boots
Ch. Timmies Sunshine Candy
Iowana's Penny Boots
Int.Ch.DeMent'sHandsomeCrusader
Miss Fortune
Ch. Ace's Cover Girl

Ch. Star Q's Brass Buttons won the Group at Westminster in 1970.

Ch. Star Q's Pease Knuto, winning BIS under Robert Waters in 1974, handled by George Rood.

that we don't take the time to really learn about our breed, as well as to learn about dogs in general.

Patricia Erickson of California and her Patcha Kennels, bred and owned Ch. Patcha's Spectacular Star, who was the dam of seven champions, of which four were sired by Ch. Chappie's Little Stardust. Ch. Patcha's Star Van was a Best in Specialty Show winner. Tom and Connie Hunter bred and owned Ch. Hunter's Perpetual Commotion, sired by Ch. Patcha's Impressario, a Group winner and specialty winner.

Byron Munson of Byron's Bostons in California, was another individual whose interest in the Boston started in 1919 and continued throughout his life. He and his wife, Doris, produced top-winning dogs over the decades. Am-Can-Mex. Ch. Byron's Short-N-Sweet won 68 Group placements, including 12 Group ones and was the top-winning Boston for three years running. He was a grandson of Buttons N' Bows. Ch. Byron's Ruff N' Ready, another Buttons grandson, was number-three Boston in 1965, winning three Group firsts. He was a consistent sire and his greatest son was Ch. Byron's Rise N' Shine, whelped in May 1946, winner of five all-breed Bests in Show, and sixteen Group firsts. In 1963, Ch. Byron's Hide N' Seek, sired by Ch. Globe Glowing All By Himself, gained her CD title, proving that the Byron dogs were not only handsome but smart as well! Ch. Byron's T-N-T won 8 specialties, 92 breeds, 5 Group firsts and 49 Group placements. Ch. Byron's Bib-N-Tucker won an all-breed Best in Show, 5 specialties and 34 Group placements.

Having done a considerable amount of research in other breeds, I cannot help but be impressed with the number of Boston breeders who did not hesitate to either buy a dog or to use a competitor's stud dog. Too often those who are newer to a breed do not

Ch. Chappie's Little Man won BIS 7 times, 68 BOBs and 28 Group firsts, owned by Charles D. Cline. Ch. Ringside Top Perfection is his most noted offspring, owned by Anna Cornwell.

recognize the amount of effort that it has taken to produce a fine animal and feel that they can do it on their own, breeding up with what they have on hand. It takes a savvy breeder to realize that if another breeder, even a competitor, has worked for years to produce a near-perfect dog, he is farther ahead by using that dog in his breeding program than in spending the years trying to breed a dog with those traits that he admires in a competitor's dogs.

Billie Niegenfeld, a breeder and a well-known handler, bred Ch. B-B's Kim of Fellow, owned by Raphael and Celeste Schulte. He was Best of Breed at Westminster in 1960, 1961 and 1962 and also had multiple Group placements. Ch. B-B's Toya's Tanyo, owned by Tom and Jackie Enwright, was the dam of

Ch. Sir Charles the Rogue, owned by Ray Perso.

four champions and the foundation bitch of their Good Time Kennels. In addition to breeding and showing her own dogs, Billie handled many Bostons to top-winning spots for their owners.

Ch. B-B's Kim of Fellow, handled by Albert Rosenbloom, winning the Group under the famous all-breed judge Alva Rosenberg in 1960.

Ch. Montecalvo's Little Whiz II.

Ch. Montecalvo's Little Whiz II

Ch. Regardless
Ch. Iowana's Fancy Boy
Iowana's Dream Girl
Ch. Iowana's Fancy Boots
Ch. H.M.S. Timmie's Easter Boots
Ch. Timmie's Sunshine Candy
Sunshine Sugar
SIRE: Ch. Iowana's Royalty Boots
Ch. Royal Handsome
Ch. DeMent's Handsome Crusader
Ch. Pageboy's Royalty Kaye
Miss Fortune
Di-B's Ace
Ch. Ace's Cover Girl
Daigler's Queen of Aces

Fallon's Lucky Chips
Ch. Montecalvo's Little Whiz
Montecalvo's Little Beauty
Buddy's Image
Escort's Yankee Boy
Ch. Montecalvo's Little Beauty II
Attention's Bit A Flash
DAM: Montecalvo's Royalty Queen II
Ch. Iowana's Fancy Boots
Ch. Iowana's Royalty Boots
Miss Fortune
Montecalvo's Little Beauty III
Escort's Yankee Boy
Ch. Montecalvo's Little Beauty II
Attention's Bit A Flash

Ray Perso, another Boston breeder who was also a multi-Group judge, owned Ch. Sir Charles the Rogue, a double grandson of Int. Ch. Grant's Royal Command. Ray and his wife finished fifteen or so champions. I have always found Ray to be not only a knowledgeable judge but a gentleman as well.

Frank Montecalvo bred Bostons for 40 years and felt that his best one was Ch. Montecalvo's Little Whiz II, a 14-pound dog who was Best of Breed at Westminster in 1964 and winner of the BTCA shows in 1962 and 1963. This was a nicely linebred dog whose pedigree was based primarily on the Iowana line.

Eva and Irwin Krueger from Iowa have been breeders since the late 1960s. Ch. Royalty's Iowana Jetaway, bred by Eva and owned by Marie Ferguson, was the number-three Boston for 1967. He was a 14-pound dog who consistently placed in the Group. He was a double grandson of Int. Ch. Grant's Royal Command and was a sound, well-balanced compact dog. The Krueger's Ch. Beau Kay's Dusty Tops Again was the sire of 11 champions and grandsire of Ch. Zodiac's Special Beau, considered to be the finest Boston Terrier up to that time. Their Ch. Unique's Royalty Kid was the dam of ten champions, including Ch. Unique's Star of Zodiac, who was the dam of Ch. Zodiac's Special Beau.

Art and Lillian Huddleston from California were very active in Bostons for many years. In addition to breeding winning Bostons, Art was a professional handler, a major collector of Boston artifacts, and a prolific writer of Boston articles for various magazines in the United States and Canada. He belonged to several regional clubs and was a life member of the BTCA for which he had served as a director. The Huddlestons purchased their first Boston in 1958, Ch. Gentleman Jim Regardless II, sire of seven champions, and that was the beginning for their Showbiz Kennels. His son, Ch. Mr. Chip Regardless, sired four champions, of which one was Ch. Showbiz Rick O Shay Romance. Romance was the sire of ten champions and the winner of many Group placements. In 1966, Lillian handled this dog from the classes to Best of Breed at the Pacific Coast Specialty.

In closing out the 1960s, mention should be made of other special dogs and their owners and/or breeders: Cora Long's Ch. Long Brat's Witch IV was an all-breed Best in Show winner; Am-Can. Ch. Aune's Brat Toughie, Am-Can. UD had an all-breed Best in Show in Canada in addition to possessing top obedience degrees in both

Ch. Showbiz Mr. Chips Regardless, owned by Arthur and Lillian Huddleston.

countries; Am-Can-Mex-Bda. Ch. Roby's Miss Kim Ann, owned by Mary Van Meter, was number-three Boston in 1964. Pearl Ruble and Shirley Canole owned Ch. Royal Show Man, sire of 13 champions; Russell Dowell's Ch. Showman's Finale Good News, sire of many champions; J. T. DeMent bred and owned Ch. DeMent's Handsome Crusader, sire of 22 champions; Mary Lou Dreher bred Ch. M. L.'s Ace High, owned by Frank Guemple, sire of 17 champions. Ch. Toy Town's High Stepping Tammy, owned by John LoPorto, had an all-breed Best in Show, 3 specialty bests and was the top-winning Boston bitch in 1968, in addition to producing 6 champions in 2 litters; Ch. Newlon's Dapper Dan, bred and owned by Dr. and Mrs. M.C. Newlon, was the top-winning Boston in 1962. His sire and grandsire was Int. Ch. Grant's Royal Commander. William Snow owned Ch. Taffy's Kid Benjamin, who was top Boston in 1965, winner of 28 Group firsts in addition to many specialty Bests in Show.

In reading through the records, one can see that even though the Boston was no longer number one or two in popularity, it was still garnering more than its share of the top wins in all-breed shows across the country. The breed continued to have its strong supporters from the "old guard" as new fanciers joined the ranks in the coming decades. The 1970s and 1980s would see even more outstanding dogs who would make major contributions to the breed.

"BENJI"

Ch. Taffy's Kid Benjamin, owned by Mr. and Mrs. William B. Snow.

Ch. Griffing's Little Chappie

Ch. Dusty's LIttle Boss
Pride of Prospect
Fisher's Dream Girl
The Little Dandy
Ch. Oh Boy of Ken Top
Boulevard Sweetheart
Bell of Prospect
SIRE: Ch. Hayes' Diplomat
Monte Carlo Handsome
Monte Carlo Captain
Fangman's Little Vamp
Mordoy's Miss Fit
D.V.M. Expectation
Gypsy Chica
Gypsy Brindy

Ch. Royal Kid Regards
Babe's Regards
Hi Hat Baby
Ch. Griffing's Little Guy
Hagerty Again Star
Griffing's Miss Hagerty Star
Kid Little Boots
DAM: Griffing's Miracle Madcap
Winna King Blink Junior
Gentleman Dandy
Ringleader's Penelope
Ch. Griffing's Little Miracle
Hagerty's Star Again
Griffing's Hagerty Star
Kids Little Boots

Banner Years: 1970s Through The 1990s

Warren Uberroth of Country Kin Kennels in New York became active in Bostons in the 1950s and bred, owned or handled 50 or so champions, in addition to being a judge of several Groups. His dogs who particularly made their mark were Ch. Country Kin Tony Award who, in eight weeks in 1984, became number-eight Boston Terrier. His full-sister from another breeding was Ch. Country Kin Carmelina, owned by Mr. and Mrs. Marc Rosen, who won over 20 Group firsts and had numerous Group placements. She was the number-one Boston bitch in 1981.

Tom and Jackie Enwright in Florida owned the Good Time Kennels. Ch. Good Time Charlie T. Brown was a multiple all-breed Best in Show winner and a five-time specialty winner, in addition to winning 18 Group firsts. In 1976 he was number-one Boston Terrier and number-ten Non-Sporting dog. He was the sire of 18 champions, including Ch. Milady Deacon of Boston, another multiple all-breed Best in Show winner.

Special mention should be made of the following: Am-Bda. Ch. Nez Pousse's Wright Choice, owned by Helen Rood, was a top-winning Boston in 1971; Ch. Bonnie's Show-N-Tell, owned by Doris Munson, won five Group firsts and had numerous Group placements; Yvette Gulledge owned the stud dogs Ch. Williams Velvet Blue and Ch. Williams Command Stormboy. Anthony Antolics and Jose Negron owned Am-Can. Ch. Simms Hi Hope Mr. Hobo, sire of 11 champions; Karen and Bob Milham of BoK's Kennels owned and bred Ch. Bo-K's Nu Masterpiece of Model, sire of 11 champions.

Linda and Jim Alexander of Georgia bred over 20 champions within 10 years or so. Their foundation bitch, Ch. Country Kin Pic-A-Dillie, whom they purchased from the Uberroths, was the dam of four champions. Ch. Alexander's Polka Dot was top brood bitch in 1984, with three of her offspring finishing their championship during the year, with a total of five champions to her credit.

Betty Swick of KimKev Kennels in Colorado has owned Bostons for over 60 years and has bred them for over 40 years. She owned the second top-producing bitch, Ch. Showman's Lovely Debbie. Debbie has several Bests of Breed and Group placements and produced eight champion offspring. She was bred the first time to Ch. KimKev's Country Gentleman, and the following two breedings were to Ch. Zodiac's Special Beau. Her last breeding was to Ch. Maestro's Perhaps Luv O'KimKev. The eight champions included Ch. KimKev's All American Girl who was number-six Boston in 1983 and 1984, and her sister, Ch. KimKev's Kalamity Jane, also a top-ten Boston in 1984 and 1985. Ch. KimKev's Jennifer was in the top ten in 1985, 1986 and in second place in 1987. Each of the eight offspring produced champions, many top winners in their day. Betty wrote,

Ch. Staley's El-Bo's Showman, the all-time top producer and sire of at least 65 champions. Owned, bred and handled by Michael Staley.

Ch. Staley's El-Bo Showman

Ch.Moore'sHappyGoLucky
Ch. Bejays Happy Jim Dandy
Bejays Ringside Happiness
Ch. Bejays Jim Dandys Happy Guy
Ch.Burnett'sSpecialTop-Step
Ch. Danlin's Soda Pop
Patcha's Starlight
SIRE: El-Bo's Rudy Is A Dandy
Byrmar'sFascinatingKid
Ch. McGee's Jason Of Sacto
Burnett'sSpecialDelight
Ch. El-Bo's Miss Liberty Belle
Chappie's Deluxe Model
Buttons-N-Bows Miss
Bewitching Miss

Ch. Da-Bo's Special Command
Ch. Unique's Royalty Kid
Royalty's Unique Imp
Ch. Circus' Candy Man
Ch. Unique's Special Beau
Circus Cotton Candy
Showman's Special Candidate
DAM: Ch. Zodiac's War Witch
Ch. Grant's Royal Command Again
Bar None's Iowana Gentleman
Ch.Iowana's'sBlackVelvetBonnie
Stormy Of Bar None
Ch. Victor of Bar None
Tempest Of Bar None
Chipper's Star Twinkle

"Good begets good if you breed them right."

Mrs. Walter Jefford, a well-known figure in the dog fancy, bought one of her first Bostons from Harry Clasen, Ch. Clasen's Elegant Lady, winner of the National Specialty show in 1968. She co-owned this dog with Michael Wolfe, who usually handled her dogs. Two bitches that did particularly well in the ring were Ch. Jefford's Abigail and Ch. Jefford's Constance, both all-breed Best in Show winners. Abigail's and Constance's dam was Ch. Jefford's Bunny, a top-producing bitch with nine champion offspring. When Mrs. Jefford decided to concentrate on Pekingese, Mr. Wolfe took the Bostons and started the Albelarm Kennels. In the early 1980s, Ch. Albelarm Rather Special and Ch. Albelarm Special Too were both all-breed Best in Show winners.

Ch. Clasen's Junior Miss, owned by Mrs. Walter M. Jeffords, Jr. of New York City.

Honore and Marc Rosen from New Jersey had several outstanding dogs, purchasing their first Boston Terrier from Harry Clasen, Am-Can. Ch. Clasen's Campus Kid. They purchased Ch. Jeffords Sherlock Holmes, and later added Ch. Jefford's Minute Man to their kennel, a dog with uncropped ears who finished in nine shows. Later they owned Am-Can. Ch. Dan Jee's I'm Suzi Too, who had a Group placement from the classes. As a special, she won 6 Group firsts and had 22 Group placements. In 1979, Country Kin Carmelina was added and proved to be an outstanding bitch. She won five Group firsts and had multiple best in specialty show wins. She was number-two Boston Terrier bitch in 1981, and number-seven in 1982 and 1983. Both Mrs. Rosen and her winning Bostons looked extremely smart in the *Boston Bulletin* pictures!

From Ottawa, Canada comes Agincourt Bostons, owned by Dr. Murray and Eleanor Heit. Am-Can. Ch. Royalyork's Duke of Agincourt was a great-grandson of Ch. Chappie's Little Stardust. Int. Ch. Heat's Dusty Wee Dodie, also out of Stardust, was a natural whelper, of which Vincent Perry said, "her head is the very study of the breed standard." Am-Can. Ch. Agincourt Kall Me Honey won the BTCA's George E. Phillips trophy, and Am-Can. Ch. Agincourt Sweet Charity was a Canadian all-breed Best in Show winner.

Charles Schmidt from Indianapolis owned several top-winning dogs from the late 1970s and 1980s. Ch. Rowdy Dowdy of Romance, bred by Mrs. Rose Culter, had multiple best in specialty show wins in 1982 through 1985. He was handled to ten all-breed Bests in Show by Ronnie Cobb. Ch. Alsanas Tugs Perfection was the top-winning Boston bitch from 1977 through 1979, bred by Alice Misak and handled by Marie Ferguson and Donald Foral.

In 1983, Carl Gomes, Boston Terrier handler and editor of the *Boston Bulletin* wrote: "The year has been a glorious period for Boston Terriers. The breed has progressed to the point where most judges give us a second look in Group competition. Our breeders have toiled unceasingly to improve conformation and character and it is our good fortune to reap the successes of their labor." He mentions specifically the following dogs who were doing exceptional winning: Ch. El-Bo's Rudy Is A Dandy; Ch. Milady Deacon of Boston; Ch. Albelarm Rather Special; Ch. Zodiac's Special Beau; Ch. Rowdy Dowdy of Romance; Ch. Unique Pleasure Lacy; and Ch. Country Kin Carmelina. He ends his article: "Without a doubt, 1982 has been our best in many years. The first six Boston Terriers gained over 1000 points in Non-Sporting Group competition and we can now boast of four Best in Show winners."

Bob and Eleanor Candland of California bred, owned and handled the great Ch. El-Bo's Rudy Is A Dandy whelped May 1981. A wonderful campaigner, Rudy won 16 all-breed Bests in Show, in addition to winning many specialties. He won 172 Bests of Breed and was left out of Group placement only 17 times. He had correct balance and sound movement, in addition to being a true showman. He

Ch, Staley's El-Bo's Showman, winning his first all-breed BIS under Mrs. M. Walton, handled by owner-breeder, Michael Staley.

was winner of the National Specialty in 1989 and was number-one Boston in 1981 through 1983. He is the sire of 58 champions, including Ch. Staley's El-Bo's Showman, also a multiple Best in Show winner and the sire of 65 champions. One of Showman's sons was Ch. Justamere's Showman Deja Vu, sire of 41 champions to date, including a Best in Show winner. To come across a line of winners like this, in any breed, is truly exciting! One cannot ignore the old axioms, ""Like begets like" and "Quality begets quality."

Dr. Robert and Jill Ritchey of Sunwoods Kennels in Ohio purchased Milady Deacon of Boston from Tom Enwright. She quickly gained her championship, handled by Jerry Rigden. She was number-one Boston bitch in 1982 and 1983 and number-two Boston Terrier both years. She won 4 all-breed Bests in Show and 32 Groups and once

won a Group 3 weeks prior to whelping a litter of 6! The Ritchey's Ch. Alexander's Star Reward was the sire of many champions. Having bred many champions over the years, Mrs. Ritchey was named "Breeder of the Year" by the BTCA in 1985.

Bob Breum's Ch. Zodiac's Special Beau was considered to be one of the best showing and producing Bostons of the time. Bred by Juanita Camp of Zodiac Kennels, Juanita realized early on that Bob Breum could do more for this dog than she would be able to and promptly sent him to live with Bob in Omaha. Whelped in 1978, Beau won 10 all-breed Bests in Show, many specialty shows and sired 41 champions, of which 5 were top-ten winners. He was stud dog of the year for three consecutive years. Although his life was short, about five years, his impact upon the breed through his progeny has been

Am-Can. Ch. Justamere's Showman Deja Vu, winner of three specialty bests from the veterans class. "Simon" is owned by Joanne Hearst and bred and handled by Ann McCammon. Judge, Marjorie Cornell.

Ch. Zodiac's Special Beau, whelped 1978, bred by Juanita Camp and owned by Robert L. Breum. He was sired by Ch. Unique's Special Beau out of Ch. Unique's Star of Zodiac. This headstudy graced the cover of The Boston Terrier by Anna Katherine Nicholas.

Ch. Zodiac's Special Beau sired at least 38 champions, won 10 all-breed BISs, 9 specialties, and 38 Group firsts.

Ch. Zodiac's Special Beau

Ch. Tops Again Happy Prince
Ch. Dusty Tops Again Special
Tops Again Stylish Lady
Ch. Beau Kay's Dusty Tops Again
Ch. Beau Kay's Royal Command
Ch. Royalty Gay Beau Kay
Ch. Royalty's Gay Patricia
SIRE: Ch. Unique's Special Beau
Ch. Da-Bo's Special Command
Ch. Iowana's Special Flash
Iowana's Fancy Dream Doll
Unique's Royalty Command
Ch. Beau Kay's Royal Command
Ch. Royalty's Unique Command
Ch. Royalty's Gay Imp Regardless

Ch. Grant's Royal Command
Ch. Da-Bo's Special Command
Ch. Iowana's Boots Fashionette
Ch. Unique's Royalty's Kid
Beau Kay's Gay Special
Royalty's Unique Imp
Ch. Royalty's Unique Command
DAM: Ch. Unique's Star of Zodiac
Ch. Royale Showman
Ch. Victor of Bar None
Ch. Christina of Bar None CD
Vogel's Velvet Cover Girl
Bar None's Iowana Gentleman
Melissa of Bar None
Bouncy Gee Gee

Ch. Zodiac's Special Warrior, owned by Mildred Gentry, winning under breeder-judge Vincent G. Perry

tremendous. Some of his offspring of special note are: Ch. Bar None's Fayme, multi-specialty winner; Ch. Zodiac's Special Warrior; Ch. Zodiac's Star Brand; Ch. Maestro's Sophie's Choice, winner of 12 Group firsts and number-one Boston in 1985. Since Bob was from Omaha and I from Minneapolis, I visited with him at many shows and to me, Bob and his Bostons always made the perfect picture: sharp, smart, confident, handsome, perfectly turned out—a total matching of handler and dog and both of them gentlemen to a tee.

Ed and Cindy Galor of Pleasure Kennels in Illinois bred and owned Am-Can. Ch. Unique's Pleasure Lacy, who was in the top-ten Bostons for five consecutive years. She won 18 specialties in addition to winning the Group 14 times. Mr. Gomes wrote that she was "a real charmer." Her sire was Ch. Unique's Royalty Kid, winner of ten specialties, and her dam was Ch. Rhett's Honest Pleasure, also a specialty winner.

Michael and Beverly Staley bred and owned Ch. Staley's El-Bo's Showman, son of the great Ch. El-Bo's Rudy Is A Dandy and out of Ch. Zodiac's War Witch, dam of five champions. He won his first all-breed Best in Show at the age of one year, owner-handled. Winner of the National Specialty show in 1985, he was the number-one Boston for 1985, winning multiple all-breed Bests in Show. He is the sire of over 65 champions, claiming him the title of all-time top producer. Ch. Staley's El-Bo's Showgirl, also owned by the Staleys, was the first Boston Terrier to be produced from frozen sperm.

Julius and Willie Martell of Kansas City bred Ch. Maestro's Billy Whiz Bang, co-owned with Bob Breum, and a Best in Show winner. Ch. Maestro's Sophie's Choice, out of Beau, and owned by Joseph and Mary Alice Niebauer, had 12 Group firsts and 43 Group placements. He sired 15 champions. In 1985, the Martells had three dogs of their breeding in the top-ten Boston list: Ch. Maestro's Sophie's Choice, Ch. Maestro's Billy Whiz Bang and Ch. Maestro's Kool Kid Miff, who was also the sire of 15 champions.

Edwin Luther of Quality Hill Kennel of California owned the most titled Boston Terrier in the world, in addition to being Mr. Luther's most beloved dog and favorite traveling companion...Ch. Chahary Crown Prince, winner of multiple specialty and Group firsts. His numerous titles are: American, Bermudan, Canadian, Mexican, Puerto Rican, Venezuelan, South American and International

Ch. Staley's El-Bo's Showgirl was the first Boston Terrier produced from frozen semen. Owned by Michael Staley.

Champion—very impressive indeed! In addition to Prince, Mr. Luther owned the most titled female Boston Terrier—Am-Mex-PR. Ch. Quality Hill Royal Princess.

Bob and Pat Stone from San Jose, California owned Ch. Stone's Bo Dusty La Lorr's, bred by Stephanie Nielson of Phoenix. Bob handled Dusty to his championship in 1985, and respected breeder-judge Emil Klinckhardt advised

Ch. Stone's Bo Dusty La Lorrs, owned by Bob and Pat Stone of San Jose, California. He has won 2 all-breed BISs, 22 Group firsts and 10 specialties.

Ch. Sabe's Unique Choice ROM, bred and owned by Ron and Sharon Saberton, a top-ten Boston in 1983. He was sired by Ch. Unique's Judges Choice out of Ch. Sabe's Unique Amanda.

Sharon Saberton from Missouri has done very well with her dogs: Ch. Sabe's Unique Choice, sired by Ch. Unique's Judges Choice, won many specialty shows, as well as multiple Group placements. He has sired many champions and was a top Boston in 1985. Ch. Sabe's Gold Dust was named the "Puppy of the Year" by the Boston Terrier Club of America in 1985. He was a specialty winner and had multiple Group placements. Gold Dust was owned by Sharon and Trudy Sample and was sired by Ch. Staley's Elbo's

them to take him home and let him enjoy his puppy times before bringing him out as a special. Alvin Lee, Sr. handled Dusty from March 1986 to December 1987, with the following impressive show record: 138 Bests of Breed, 22 Group firsts with an additional 60 Group placements, 2 all-breed Bests in Show, 10 Bests in Specialty Show, including 1986 National. Dusty was the number one Boston Terrier in 1986 and 1987. In addition, in 1988 he was the first recipient of the Kal-Kan Pedigree award. Pat wrote, "To accomplish this with a little dog you loved with all your heart is a dream come true." A good reminder that we all got our first dog because we wanted a pet to love. It's still most important to have a pet to love, and the wins are just the frosting on the cake.

Ch. Sabe's Gold Dust ROM, bred by Ron and Sharon Saberton, and owned with Trudy Sample. Breeder-judge, Emil Klinckhardt. He was sired by Ch. Staley's El-Bo's Showman ROM out of Ch. Sabe's Modern Millie ROM

Showman. The Saberton's Ch. Beacon's Destin To-Be By Sabe was a specialty Best of Breed winner from the six to nine month puppy class and had multiple Group placements.

Ch. Beacon's Do-Go Sunny of Sabe, bred by Marian Sheehan and Mary Jo Schreimann, was number-one Boston Terrier, all systems, in 1991 and number-one in all-breed systems 1992. His record included 181 Bests of Breed, 46 Group placements and 19 Group firsts. He was Best of Breed at Wesminster in 1991, Best of Breed at the 1991 Purina Invitational and Best of Breed and Group second at the 1992 Purina Invitational. At the American Kennel Club National Invitational in 1992 he was Best of Breed and Group third. In addition to his impressive show wins, he has sired at least 25 champions. His champion offspring include Ch. Kap's Beau by Sunny, all-breed Best in Show winner, bred by Kent and Jane Peters, and Ch. Roobarbs Hot Diggity, a multiple Group winner. Six champions were produced when bred to Ch. Gimp's Hot Roobarb.

Janet and Richard Rees from Overland Park, Kansas noted that all of their Bostons go back to the great Ch. Zodiac's Special Beau. Their Ch. Rees' Classic American Pride is well known and loved throughout the country. She was bred only once, producing Ch. Rees' Pride's American Charmer and she, in turn, has produced three beautiful Bostons.

Ch. Beacon's Destined to Be by Sabe, breeder-handled by Sharon Saberton under breeder-judge Michael Staley. Trophy presenter, Paul Schwartz, old-time Boston breeder and editor of the breed magazine in the early 1900s.

Ch. Beacon's Do-Go Sunny of Sabe ROM, bred by Marian Sheehan and Mary Jo Schreimann and owner-handled by Ron and Sharon Saberton. He is the winner of 16 specialties, sired by Ch. Do-Go Georges Buddy of Rudy ROM out of Ch. Beacon's Tiny Darling ROM.

Ann McCammon of Terre Haute, Indiana sees herself as a relative newcomer, starting to seriously breed in the mid-1980s. With beginner's luck—and this proves that it can happen!—Ann and Jim had a star in their very first litter...Ch. Justamere's Showman Deja Vu., sired by Ch. Staley's El-Bo's Showman, and now owned by Joanne Hearst. Deja Vu's show record is impressive even as an old timer, with three specialty Bests of Breed from the Veterans class, at the ages of seven, eight and nine. In addition, at nine years of age, he received first Award of Merit at the 1996 Westminster show. He was the 1990 Pedigree top Boston of the year and he is the sire of no fewer than 41 champions. One of his Group winning get is Ch. O.J. First Class Fortune Cooky, the first Boston bitch to go all-breed Best in Show in over a decade. She is owned by Joanne Hearst and Ann and was bred by Ola Jeanne McCollough. Unfortunately, Cooky died at an early age of an incident involving herbicide inhalation. Ann has been a tremendous assistance to me in the writing of this book as she has been the liaison between the BTCA and myself. My thanks to her for sharing her knowledge, her time and her love of the breed.

Maxine Uzoff from Houston, Texas bred Ch. Oui's Hi Step'n Coca Cola Cowboy, CD, who achieved his championship with all points won from the Bred by Exhibitor class with four majors, a very nice, and difficult, achievement. He has sired no fewer than ten champions, two of which have been in the top-ten Boston Terrier list. Ch. C.G's Hi Stepn Oui Tambourine, owned by Carol and Gary Moore, was the number-one Boston bitch in 1990.

Ch. Rees' Classic American Pride, whelped 1987, breeder-owner-handled by Richard and Janet Rees, winning under breeder-judge Bob Candland. She was sired by Ch. Maestro's He Be A Doozy out of Ch. KimKev's American Classic.

Ch. WC's Victoria's Secret of Oui, bred and owned by Suzanne Maxine Uzoff with W.C. Billinsley, sired by Ch. Oui's Hi Stepn Coca Cola Cowboy CD, ROM, was the number-one bitch in 1995 and number-two Boston.

Ch. WC's Mon Ami of Oui, top-winning bitch in 1994 and top-ten in 1993 and 1994, bred by S. Maxine Uzoff and owned with W.C. Billingsley. Handled by Rod Merry.

breed Best Puppy in Show. Am-Can. Ch. Abacab's Total Eclipse was the winner of the Boston Terrier Club of Canada and a multiple Group winner. He finished his American championship with three five-point majors. Am-Can. Ch. Abacab's Sunday Solitaire received an Award of Merit at the BTCA National specialty and finished with three specialty majors, in addition to winning three all-breed Best Puppy in Show, all owner-handled. Can.

Ch. W.C.'s Victoria's Secret of Oui has won 6 Group firsts, 4 Bests in Specialty Show and 29 Group placements. Owned by Maxine and co-owned with W. C. Billingsley, she won 64 Bests of Breed and was a BTCA Award of Merit winner in 1995 and 1996. Coca Cola Cowboy's double granddaughter, Ch. W.C.'s Mon Ami of Oui, co-owned by Maxine and Billingsley, was the number-one Boston Terrier bitch in 1994, winning 6 specialties and 41 Bests of Breed.

Robin Cameron and Peter Hicks, from Ontario, Canada, have done very well with their dogs. Am-Can. Ch. Abacab's Simply Irresistible, owned and bred by Robin and Peter, is a Group and specialty winner with multiple Group placements. He was number-one Boston in Canada in 1991. Am-Can. Ch. Top Shelf Crackerjack ROM, bred by Tom and Suzanne Ghaster, is the sire of several Group and specialty winners. AmCan. Ch. Abacab's Midnite Madness, a multiple Group winner, has won two all-

Ch. Rowdy Dowdy of Romance, owned by Charles Schmidt and handled by Ronnie Cobb.

Ch. O.J. First Class Fortune Cooky at two years of age, winning BIS under Esme Treen and handled by Ann McCammon, who co-owns with Joanne Hearst.

Ch. Abacab's Bold Mischief Encore, ROM was the dam of five American champions and eight Canadian champions. Am-Can. Ch. Bold Mischief at Tijuana, TT won two all-breed Bests in Show and was number-one Boston in Canada in 1988.

Before closing out the 1980s, let's mention: Ch. Howell's Sage 'n Sand Tuxedoman, sire of many champions, bred and owned by Norma and Bud Howell; Ch. Rowdy Dowdy of Romance, winner of four Bests in Show; Andy Turner, breeder of Ch. Tops Again Duke of Regards, sire of 21 champions, Ch. Dusty Tops Again Special, sire of 14 champions, and Ch. Tops Again Gay Pepper, sire of 14 champions; Ch. Zodiac's Special Warrior, ROM, sired by Ch. Zodiac's Special Beau and out of Ch. Zodiac's War Witch, finished in five shows at the age of ten months, said by Vincent Perry to be one of the best he had ever judged and unfortunately killed in an accident at three years of age.

In addition, Norman and Marilyn Randall have produced a number of fine Bostons and Norman was the first Boston breeder to become a certified professional handler.

Time can only tell who the breeders of the future will be, who will have an impact to the extent that the Hagerty, Kingway, Globe, Iowana, Clasen, Showbiz Kennels and others have had. The breed is in good condition, and through the efforts and dedication of the breeders of the future, it will remain as such.

Ch. Sage'N Sand Sally J, owned and bred by Florence Brooks. She was sired by Maria's Bubby Boy out of Sage'N Sand Piper.

Ch. Bo-K's Masterpiece of Model ROM, owned by Bob and Karen Milham.

Int-Am-Dutch-Ger-Bel-Lux-Monaco-French-Can. Ch. Oranjelust Royal Showman, bred by C.J. Koudijs and owned by Harriet Kolias and Ann Spurling Roark. He is the sire many champions. His sire was Int-Dutch-Ger-Bel-Swiss SunGlo's Pilot Light out of Int-Dutch-Ger-Lux. Ch. Oranjelust Annie Laurie.

Ch. Unique's Star of Zodiac, whelped 1977, bred by Juanita Camp and owned by Earl and Mildred Gentry. She is the dam of Ch. Zodiac's Special Beau. Her sire was Ch. Unique's Royalty Kid out of Ch. Vogel's Velvet Cover Girl.

Ch. Alsanas Tugs Perfection, owned by Charles Schmidt, was the top-winning bitch from 1977 through 1979.

Am-Ber. Ch. Chahary de Fantaisie Veneza CD, owned by Edwin R. Luther.

The first champion for Norman and Marilyn Randall, Ch. Ancor's Medaille Command, known as Ginger.

Ch. Ancor's Royale Warrior, owned by Norman and Marilyn Randall, became their second champion. He was known as Boomer.

Ch. Zodiac's Special Warrior.

Ch. Pilot's Star Steppin' Am-Mex. CD, an outstanding sire of the 1960s owned by Frankie Gates.

Ch. Torchy's Good News of SunGlo, bred by Harriet Kolias and Ann Spurling and owned by Lucille Sheets. She is the sire of Ch. Good Time Charlie T. Brown, a number-one Boston in the 1980s.

Aust-NZ. Ch. Sterlin Silva of Rossdhu, owned by Colquohouns of New Zealand.

Int-Dutch-German-Swiss. Ch SunGlo's Pilot Light, an all-breed BIS winner in Europe, bred by Harriet Kolias and Ann Spurling and owned by Mrs. C.J. Koudys of the Netherlands. He was the sire of many champions including Int. Ch. Oranjelust Royal Showman.

Ch. Kennedy's Boston Pops at eight months of age, owned by Vicki and Sarah Kennedy.

Ch. Silver Frost of Rossdhu, sired by Sgt. Pepper of Dee-Ross out of Aust-NZ Ch. Sterlin Silver of Rossdhu, bred by the Colquohouns.

Carol Enwright handles for owner Mary Lou Anderson at the Portland anniversary show.

Champions of the Americas and Am-Can-Mex-PR. Ch. Quality Hill Royal Princess, bred, owned, and handled by Edwin Luther.

Ch. Oui's Hi Step'n Coca Cola Cowboy CD, ROM, breeder-owned by S. Maxine Uzoff, the sire of multiple champions.

Ch. Staley's Trudy Is a Dandy, litter sister to Ch. Staley's El-Bo's Showman.

Ch. KimKev's Charming Vixon, owned by Edna Swift and bred by Betty Swick. Sired by Ch. Maestro's Perhaps Luv O'KimKev out of Ch. Showman's Lovely Debbie.

Int-Am-Ber-Can-Mex-PR-Vez-SoAm. Ch. Chahary Crown Prince, owned by Edwin Luther.

Ch. Bar None's Elegance, whelped 1983, bred by Robert Breum and owned by Richard and Janet Rees. BTCA National Specialty best brood bitch 1988. Sired by Ch. Sabe's Lucky Punch out of Ch. Bar None's Fayme.

Brandy's Little Britches, owned by Bruce and Sandy Crook.

Jondan's Imagine, bred and owned by John and Sue Milner.

Ch. Bar None's Tom Sawyer ROM, whelped 1984, bred by Robert Breum and Gary Decker and owned by Earl and Mildred Gentry. Sired by Ch. Maestro's Billy Whiz Bang out of Ch. Bar None's Fayme.

Ch. Bo-K's Rocky Balboa, owned by Bob and Karen Milham.

Ch. Agincourt Honey Bonne was the first Boston Terrier for owners, Mr. and Mrs. David Montgomery.

Ch. Bo-K's Dandy Aristocrat owned by Bob and Karen Milham

Ch. Sabe's Sara of Toy Town, bred by Ron and Sharon Saberton and owned by John LoPorto. Sired by Ch. Staley's El-Bo's Showman ROM out of Ch. Sabe's Modern Millie ROM.

Bo-K's Polished Model, handled by owner-breeder, Bob Milham, winning under judge Thomas Conway.

Sage'N Sand Bowtie Bingo and Sage'N Sand Lace Britches, owner-handled by Bud and Norm Howell, bred by Florence Brooks. These two seven-month-old littermates were sired by Ch. Sage'N Sand Have Tux Can Travel out of SunGlo's Kandi Kid. Judge, Lois McMannus.

Ch. What's Up Tiger Lily, winning under breeder-judge Vincent G. Perry, handled by S. Maxine Uzoff.

Bo-K's Brandy Belle Starr, owner-handled by Bob Milham, winning sweepstakes under breeder-judge Anthony Antolics.

Best brace at the 1988 BTCA National went to Ch. Rees' Classic American Pride and Ch. Rees' Captivating Cameo, breeder-owner-handled by Janet Rees. Judge, Emil Klinckhardt. BTCA President, Joan Eckert.

Best team at the 1988 BTCA National went to Janet Rees's quartet: Ch. Rees' Vanity Fair Elegance, Ch. Rees' Amber Elegance, Ch. Rees' Classic American Pride and Ch. Rees' Captivating Cameo. Judge, Emil Klinckhardt. BTCA President, Joan Eckert.

Ch. Rees' Amber Elegance, whelped 1985, owner-handled by Richard Rees, winning under breeder-judge Maryann Caruso. Sired by Ch. Maestro's Billy Whiz Bang out of Ch. Bar None's Elegance.

Four generations of Oui champions: Oui's Hi Stepn Coca Cola Cowboy with his daughter Ch. Oui's Lil Miss Brigitte Bardot, with her son Ch. Oui's First Class Frequent Flyer, with his son Ch. Oui's Hi Stepn Star Man of WC.

Ch. Jondan's Those Dandy Bubbles, owner-handled by Sue Milner, winning under judge Thomas Conway.

The Boston Terrier Club of America

The Boston Terrier Club of America, a non-profit organization, was founded in 1891 and was one of the early breed clubs to be recognized by the American Kennel Club. The objective of the club, as stated in the constitution, is:

a. To encourage and promote quality in the breeding of pure-bred Boston Terriers, and to do all possible to bring their natural qualities to perfection;

b. To encourage the organization and development of affiliated Boston Terrier clubs in those localities where there are sufficient fanciers of the breed to meet the requirements of the American Kennel Club;

c. To urge members and breeders to accept the Standard of the Breed as approved by the American Kennel Club as the only Standard of excellence by which Boston Terriers shall be judged;

d. To do all in its power to protect and advance the interest of the breed and to encourage sportsmanlike competition at dog shows and obedience trials;

The Boston Terrier Club of America National Specialty 1992, stud dog class judged by Mrs. Connie Hunter. Top stud dog, Am-Can. Ch. Justamere's Showman Deja Vu, with offspring Am-Can. Ch. Maximillian's Earl the Pearl, Am-Can. Ch. Maximillian's Duchess Wine, Ch. Maximillian's Surely By Simon and Ch. Justamere's Seraphim On High.

The all-time top producer, Ch. Staley's El-Bo's Showman, owned by Michael Staley.

e. To conduct sanctioned matches, specialty shows and obedience trials under the rules of the American Kennel Club.

At the present time, membership consists of approximately 500 individuals who live throughout America, as well as in Canada, England, New Zealand, Philippines, Sweden and Zimbabwe. True to its name, for nearly 100 years, the club was centered in Boston, Massachusetts, where the breed was founded. In 1985 the club held its first specialty show outside of Massachusetts and since that time the national show has "floated" around country. In 1991 the national show returned to its origins for the centennial show at Hyannis, Massachusetts, where 261 Boston Terriers were entered for the gala event.

If you apply for membership you will be required to complete an application form and have the sponsorship of two BTCA members in good standing. In addition, you are expected to abide by the club's Code of Ethics and by-laws. The application will ask if you own any breeds other than Boston Terriers and if you belong to any other kennel clubs. Most importantly, you will be asked why you are interested in belonging to the Boston Terrier Club of America. Along with your application for membership, you will also be asked to sign the BTCA Code of Ethics.

The Code of Ethics is established in accordance with the objectives of the Boston Terrier Club of America. It is presented as a guideline for the use of Boston Terrier Club members when buying, breeding, selling, and exhibiting Boston Terriers. When you sign the Code of Ethics, you are pledging to abide by the constitution and the by-laws of the club. You will breed your bitches with the intention of improving the breed; your dogs and bitches will be healthy and free from dis-qualifying genetic faults. In addition, you will keep accurate records, sales agreements and you will furnish records to each buyer. You will refuse to sell a Boston to a buyer who cannot or will not provide evidence of ability to properly care for the animal, and you will not sell a Boston to any commercial facility or puppy broker.

At the Minuteman BT Club, best team for 1996 was owned by Leasa Tyrrell, winning under judge Marjorie Cornell.

With membership in the BTCA, you will receive the *Coast-To-Coast* newsletter, which is published quarterly and will keep you current on the business at hand and on future events of the BTCA. Even living miles from another BTCA member, you can keep up with the news and activities of the Boston regional clubs throughout the country. Meetings are usually held on a monthly basis and programs are offered by experienced Boston owners on how to show your dog, whelp a litter of puppies, know a good Boston, or work a dog in obedience. Most of these clubs hold their own annual specialties,

Boston Terrier Club of America National Specialty, best brood bitch 1988 was Ch. Bar None's Elegance with offspring Ch. Rees' Captivating Cameo, Ch. Rees' Amber Elegance, and Ch. Rees' Vanity Fair Elegance. Judge, Emil Klinckhardt. Breeder-owners, Richard and Janet Rees.

world. All-breed clubs have education as a priority and the Boston Terrier club is no different. Articles are available for both members and for prospective Boston Terrier owners. And for those of you with computers, the BTCA has information on the Internet that is available to everyone.

Working under the authority and guidance of the American Kennel Club and the BTCA, there are presently 30 which are well attended by fanciers in the area, and sometimes attended by handlers from many miles away. Many individuals will only belong to the regional club, finding everything that they need within this Group., There is often a camaraderie and a willingness to help each other that make these clubs very special, and some members find it worthwhile to drive 150 miles or so to attend a monthly meeting.

BTCA-Affiliated Clubs

Minuteman BT Club (Massachusetts.)Lenape BT Club (New Jersey)
Tri-Angle BT Breeders Club (New Jersey)
BT Club of New York
BT Club of Western Pennsylvania
BT Club of Maryland
BT Club of Miami, Florida
Florida Suncoast BT Club
Birmingham BT Club (Alabama)
BT Club of Connecticut
BT Club of Louisville (Kentucky)
BT Club of Greater Cincinnati (Ohio)
Western BT Club, (Indiana)
Fort Wayne BT Club
BT Club of Detroit (Michigan)
Hawkeye BT Club (Iowa)
BT Club of Milwaukee (Winconsin)
Minnesota BT Club
Heartland BT Club (Missouri)
BT Club of Louisiana
Oklahoma City BT Club
North Texas BT Club (Dallas)
Greater Houston BT Club (Texas)
Valley of the Sun BT Club (Arizona)
Pasadena BT Club (California)
BT Club of San Diego County
Golden Gate BT Club
BT Club of Portland, Oregon
BT Club of Western Washington
Pacific Coast BT Club (California—non-affiliate)
Metropolitan Washington BT Club (District of Columbia)

Annual BTCA Awards

Best of Breed trophies: Fred Davis Cup; William Collins Memorial Trophy; Vincent G. Perry trophy

Best of Opposite Sex: George E. Phillips Memorial Trophy; John O'Connell Trophy

Best of Winners: Arthur R. Huddleston Memorial Trophy

Winners Dog: William J. Degan Trophy

Winners Bitch: George E. McKenna Trophy

Boston Terrier Club of America National Specialty, best brood bitch 1986 was Ch. Showman's Lovely Debbie with her two daughters Ch. KimKev's Kalamity Jane and Ch. KimKev's Jennifer, BOS that year. Judge, Leonard Myers. Owner, Betty Swick.

Within the BTCA, the membership includes those who are actively breeding and showing their dogs; those who judge not only the Boston Terrier but all Non-Sporting dogs and dogs in other Groups as well; those who have written about the Boston and dogs in general; and those who year after year work doggedly behind the scenes taking care of the club's business. There is a wide range of people whose interest and love for the Bostons bond them together, often forming friendships that last a lifetime.

In addition to the above, the Boston Terrier Club of America has been very active in rescue work. This is a network of BTCA affiliate clubs dedicated to placing unwanted or abandoned Boston Terriers in a good home. This is a well-thought-out program, run by dedicated individuals who want to see that all Boston Terriers have a loving and caring home.

For information on the BTCA or an affiliated club, write to the American Kennel Club and they will send you the name and address of the current corresponding secretary. You may also contact your local all-breed club for the locality of a regional club.

Celebrating 100 years of America's own Boston Terrier! The BTCA Centennial National Specialty 1991 took place at Hyannisport, Massachusetts, not far from the breed's birthplace!

The Standard for the Boston Terrier

Each breed approved by the American Kennel Club has a standard which gives the reader a mental picture of what the specific breed should look like. All reputable breeders strive to produce animals that will meet the requirements of the standard. Many breeds were developed for a specific purpose, i.e., hunting, retrieving, going to ground, coursing, guarding, and herding. The Boston Terrier, like a few other breeds, was eventually developed to be a companion dog and a house dog.

Little has changed since 1910 when Edward Axtell wrote, "The standard adopted by the Boston Terrier Club in 1900 was the result of earnest, sincere, thoughtful deliberations of as conservative and conscientious a body of men as could anywhere be gotten together. Nothing was done in haste, the utmost consideration was given to every detail and it was a thoroughly matured, and practically infallible guide by men who were genuine lovers of the dog for its own sake and who were perfectly familiar with the breed from its start."

Am-Can. Ch. Ancoramn's Special Brandywine, owned by Norman and Marilyn Randall.

In addition to having dogs that *look* like a proper Boston Terrier, the standard assures that our dogs will have the personality, disposition and intelligence that is sought for in a companion dog.

Standards were originally written by fanciers who had a love and a concern for the breed. They knew that the essential characteristics of the Boston Terrier were unlike any other breed and that care must be taken that these characteristics were maintained through the generations.

As time passed and breeders became more aware that certain areas of the dog needed a better description or more definition, breeders would meet together and work out a new standard.

Ch. Justamere's Showman Deja Vu, bred by Jim and Ann McCammon and owned by Joanne Hearst.

However, standards for any breed are never changed on a whim and serious study and exchange between breeders take place before any move is made.

The standard is continually studied by serious dog breeders and judges. However, the reading and interpretation of the standard are subjective and open to interpretation by the individual who is reading it. It is important that every breeder and every judge of Boston Terriers study the standard carefully in addition to seeing as many Boston Terriers as possible. Through time and study, a picture will form in the mind of what constitutes a correct Boston.

In time the standard became more detailed and what started out to be a statement of perhaps a half page, grew to be much longer and more detailed. The original standard created a dog that was more substantial than the present dog...weight was divided into three classes, *15 pounds and under; 25 pounds and under; 36 pounds and under.* The present standard gives the top weight as not to exceed 25 pounds. The eyes, which are so important to give a correct Boston look, were described in 1900 as: *wide apart, dark and soft, not "goggle" eyed.* Note how specific the present standard is to the eye color, shape and the set. The color of the dog has also changed. The 1900 standard states: *any color, except black, mouse, or liver; brindle and white, brindle or whole white are the colors most preferred.* The present standard gives the disqualifying color, in addition to the required markings, which are essential in the Boston. In addition, the current standard has a section on temperament, stating, "the breed has an excellent disposition and a high degree of intelligence," which is essential for the purpose of the breed—the outstanding companion dog!

The present standard, as revised by the BTCA membership and approved by the American Kennel Club, February 1990:

GENERAL APPEARANCE

The Boston Terrier is a lively, highly intelligent, smooth coated, short headed, compactly built, short-tailed, well balanced dog, brindle, seal or black in color and evenly marked with white. The head is in proportion to the size of the dog and the expression indicates a high degree of intelligence.

The body is rather short and well knit, the limbs strong and neatly turned, the tail is short and no feature is so prominent that the dog appears badly proportioned. The dog conveys an impression of determination, strength and activity, with style of a high order; carriage easy and graceful. A proportionate combination of "Color and White Markings" is a particularly distinctive feature of a representative specimen.

"Balance, Expression, Color and White Markings" should be given particular consideration in determining the relative value of GENERAL APPEARANCE to other points.

SIZE, PROPORTION, SUBSTANCE

Weight is divided by classes as follows: Under 15 pounds; 15 pounds and under 20 pounds; 20 pounds and not to exceed 25 pounds. The length of leg must balance with the length of body to give the Boston Terrier its striking square appearance. The Boston Terrier is a sturdy dog and must not appear to be either spindly or coarse. The bone and muscle must be in proportion as well as an enhancement to the dog's weight and structure. Fault: Blocky or chunky in appearance.

Influence of Sex In a comparison of specimens of each sex, the only evident difference is a slight refinement in the bitch's conformation.

HEAD

The *skull* is square, flat on top, free from wrinkles, cheeks flat, brow abrupt and the stop well defined. The ideal Boston Terrier *expression* is alert and kind, indicating a high degree of intelligence. This is a most important characteristic of the breed. The *eyes* are wide apart, large and round and dark in color. The eyes are set square in the skull and the outside corners are on a line with the cheeks as viewed from the front. Disqualify: Eyes blue in color or any trace of blue. The *ears* are small, carried erect, either natural or cropped to conform to the shape of the head and situated as near to the corners of the skull as possible.

The *muzzle* is short, square, wide and deep and in proportion to the skull. It is free from wrinkles, shorter in length than in depth; not exceeding in length approximately one-third of the length of the skull. The muzzle from stop to end of the nose is parallel to the top of the skull.

The *nose* is black and wide, with a well defined line between the nostrils. Disqualify: Dudley nose.

The *jaw* is broad and square with short, regular teeth. The bite is even or sufficiently undershot to square the muzzle. The chops are of good depth, but not pendulous, completely covering the teeth when the mouth is closed. Serious Fault: Wry mouth. Head Faults: Eyes showing too much white or haw. Pinched or wide nostrils. Size of ears out of proportion to the size of the head. Serious Head Faults: Any showing of the tongue or teeth when the mouth is closed.

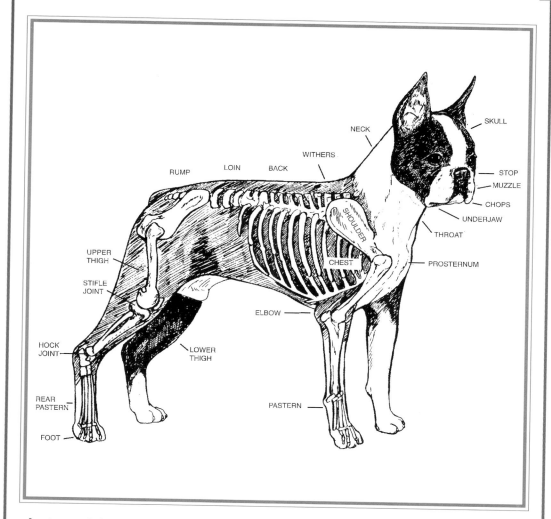

Anatomy of the Boston Terrier, illustrated by Vickie Kwasny. Courtesy of the BTCA.

Bite types.

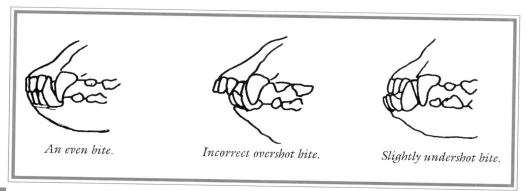

An even bite.   *Incorrect overshot bite.*   *Slightly undershot bite.*

NECK, TOPLINE AND BODY

The length of neck must display an image of balance to the total dog. It is slightly arched, carrying the head gracefully and setting neatly into the shoulders. The back is just short enough to square the body. The topline is level and the rump curves slightly to the set-on of the tail. The chest is deep with good width, ribs well sprung and carried well back to the loins. The body should appear short. The tail is set on low, short, fine and tapering, straight or screw and must not be carried above the horizontal. (Note: The preferred tail does not exceed in length more than one-quarter the distance from set-on to hock.) Disqualify: Docked tail. Body Faults: Gaily carried tail. Serious Body Faults: Roach back, sway back, slab-sided.

FOREQUARTERS

The *shoulders* are sloping and well laid back, which allows for the Boston Terrier's stylish movement. The *elbows* stand neither in nor out. The forelegs are set moderately wide apart and on a line with the upper tip of the shoulder blades. The forelegs are straight in bone with short, strong pasterns. The dewclaws may be removed. The feet are small, round and compact, turned neither in nor out, with well-arched toes and short nails. Faults: Legs lacking in substance; splay feet.

HINDQUARTERS

The thighs are strong and well muscled, bent at the stifles and set true. The hocks are short to the feet, turning neither in nor out, with a well defined hock joint. The feet are small and compact with short nails. Fault: Straight in stifle.

GAIT

The gait of the Boston Terrier is that of a sure footed, straight gaited dog, forelegs and hind legs moving straight ahead in line with perfect rhythm, each step indicating grace and power. Gait Faults: There will be no rolling, paddling, or weaving when gaited. Hackney gait. Serious Gait Faults: Any crossing movement, either front or rear.

COAT

The coat is short, smooth, bright and fine in texture.

COLOR AND MARKINGS

Brindle, seal, or black with white markings. Brindle is preferred ONLY if all other qualities are equal. (Note: SEAL DEFINED, Seal appears black except it has a red cast when viewed in the sun or bright light.) Disqualify: Solid black, solid brindle or solid seal without required markings. Gray or liver colors.

Required Markings: White muzzle band, white blaze between the eyes, white-forechest.

Desired Markings: White muzzle band, even white blaze between the eyes and over the head, white collar, white forechest, white on part or whole of fore legs and hind legs below the hocks. (Note: A representative specimen should not be penalized for not possessing "Desired Markings.") A dog with a preponderance of white on the head or body must possess sufficient merit otherwise to counteract its deficiencies.

TEMPERAMENT

The Boston Terrier is a friendly and lively dog. The breed has an excellent disposition and a high degree of intelligence, which makes the Boston Terrier an incomparable companion.

SUMMARY

The clean-cut, short backed body of the Boston Terrier, coupled with the unique characteristics of his square head and jaw, and his striking markings have resulted in a most dapper and charming American original: The Boston Terrier.

Level topline, good reach of front assembly.

INCORRECT
Crossing of front feet.

GAIT
MOVEMENT

Good movement—head on.

INCORRECT
Paddling movement.

INCORRECT
Hackney gait.

SCALE OF POINTS

General Appearance	10
Expression	10
Head (muzzle, jaw, bite, skull, stop)	15
Eyes	5
Ears	5
Neck, Topline, Body, Tail	15
Forequarters	10
Hindquarters	10
Feet	5
Color, Coat, Markings	5
Gait	10
TOTAL	100

DISQUALIFICATION

Eyes blue in color or any trace of blue.
Dudley nose.
Docked tail.
Solid black, solid brindle, or solid seal without required markings.
Gray or liver colors.

When you join the Boston Terrier Club of America you will receive a booklet entitled *The Boston Terrier : A Pictorial and Illustrated Standard*. This will give you a detailed explanation of the standard along with pictures and drawings.

To sum up the standard, Vincent Perry wrote, "His combination of curves that make a streamlined figure, his attractive color and bright white markings, and his sculptured classic head, set off as it is by his big lustrous eyes and perky ears, form a real beauty. He is every inch the aristocrat of dogdom."

Ch. Barra's Highland Lassie, breeder-owned by Elisabeth McNeil, three-time Westminster Breed winner plus over 100 other BOBs. This bitch was sired by Barra's Vinny P of Agincourt out of Barra's Irish Queen.

Ch. Classic's Special Kid K, breeder-owner handled by Carol Mohr and Carole Ann. This dog was sired by Ch. Albelarm Special Too out of Ch. Cia's Classic Sneak Preview. He has won BOB over 120 times.

Ch. Katbird's Special Edition, whelped 1995, handled by owner Susan Krouse, finishing from the puppy class.

Ch. O.J. First Class Fortune Cooky, finishing her championship under judge Charles Bordelon, owned by Joanne Hearst and Ann McCammon and bred by OlaJeanne McCollough. Cooky became the first Boston Terrier bitch to win BIS in over a decade.

Ch. Rees' Pride's American Charmer, owner-breeder-handled by Richard and Janet Rees.

Am-Can. Ch. Abacab's Simply Irresistible, bred and owned by Robin Cameron and Peter Hicks, was the number-one Boston Terrier in Canada in 1991.

Ch. Katrinea's Mr. Gentleman Jim, owned by Kathy Ford and Mary Lou Anderson.

Ch. Al-Mar's Just the Fax, owned by Pat and Sue Kennedy. Sired by Ch. Al-Mar's By Invitation Only out of Al-Mar's Dancers Delight.

Ch. Ken's Broadway Mariah, owned by Beverly Staley and Ken Roux.

Ch. J & S Hi-Flying Feisty Poncho, bred and handled by Susan Wallace, owned by Valerie Stanavage.

Ch. Maximillian's Rambunctious Brat, owned by Joanne Hearst, Barbara Bate and Pauline Nedeau.

Ch. Al-Mar's Strike A Pose, breeder-owned by Pat and Sue Kennedy. Sired by Ch. Al-Mar's Dashing Commander out of Ch. Al-Mar's Buffy of Rub'N Buff.

Ch. Maranatha Sparkle and Shine, breeder-owned by Valerie Stanavage. Sired by Ch. Maranatha Mark My Words out of Ch. Liberty Hello Luv at Maranatha.

Am-Can. Ch. Justamere's Showman Deja Vu, handled by Ann McCammon, winning Award of Merit at Westminster in 1996 under judge Norman Patton.

Ch. Garrett's Canadian Made, bred by Colleen Garrett, owner-handled by Jayne Palmer. Sired by Ch. Fourstar's Taylors Tom Son.

Above: Ch. Lux's Scarlet O'Hara of Al-Mar, owned by Nancy Lux, winning Group second at the Prescott Arizona KC.

Right: Ch. R.J.'s Sunshine Always, whelped 1992, bred and handled by Sheryl Trent and owned by Victoria Carter. Judge, Melbourne Downing.

A sunny day for Ch. Robmar's Lollipops and Roses, owned by Marian Robben, at the Palm Springs KC.

Am-Can. Ch. Abacab's Sunday Solitaire, breeder-owned by Robin Cameron and Peter Hicks. Breeder-judge, Dr. Murray Heit.

Ch. Maximillian's Masterpiece by JR, owned by Brad and Pauline Nedeau.

Ch. Steele's Ancoramn Top Gun, owned by Hazel Steele and bred by Norman and Marilyn Randall.

Juwell's Teddy Bear of KimKev, bred and handled by Judy Criswell

Ch. Juwell's Cookies and Creme, bred and shown by Judy Criswell, a litter sister to Teddy Bear.

Ch. Showman's Ravishing Ruby, owned by Michael Staley.

Ch. Rees' Captivating Cameo and Ch. Rees' Classic American Pride, winning best brace. Breeder-owners, Richard and Janet Rees.

Above: *Ch. Anchor's Special Jazz, owner-handled by Marilyn Randall.*

Upper left: *Ch. Beacon's Do-Go Sunny of Sabe ROM, owner-handled by Sharon Saberton, winning under Anne Rogers Clark. He won the BTCA National in 1991.*

Middle left: *Noted breeder, judge and author Ethel Braunstein, judging a specialty in 1990. Owner, Marian Robben.*

Ch. Rees' Classic American Pride, bred, owned and handled by Richard and Janet Rees. Judge, Leonard Myers. BTCA President, C. A. Nicks.

Characteristics and Care of the Boston Terrier

An all-American adventurer seeker, the Boston Terrier has conquered the world with his winning personality and handsome looks. This is Ch. Lux's Tom Selleck of Al-Mar.

So much has been written about the charm of a Boston Terrier that it is hard to know where to start! First, the popularity of the breed over so many decades tells one that this is a breed that has been a popular house pet, and to be a popular house pet this must be a breed that is easy to live with and easy to keep up.

In 1906, Mrs. W. E. Porter of Denver, acquired her first Boston Terrier and eventually established the well-known Kingway Kennels. She once wrote in a letter, "I believe we should push our dog as a pet...the characteristics of the breed make him ideal for a family dog. He is good tempered; he is not a tramp; he is easy to keep clean, no doggy odor; he's intelligent and good looking. We would all rather see a Boston on the neighbor's lawn or in his car than any other breed."

He is considered by all to be a true companion who is kind, gentle, affectionate and smart. He is quick to learn and eager to please. Of course, the Boston's intelligence should also be stressed and this is what makes him such a fun and fine companion. A smart

Always searching for new avenues, here's Ch. What's Up Tiger Lily and her son Ch. Oui's Hi Stepn Coca Cola Cowboy CD, ROM.

dog can often be as sensitive to his owner's moods as an individual's best friend can be. What comfort, when you are having a sad day, to have your little dog come up and put his head in your lap, telling you that "everything will be all right." ("When a man is lonely, God sends him a dog.")

His small size makes him easy to handle, easy to have in an apartment and easy to take along for a ride. You can pick him up and carry him under your arm or you can walk several of them together on a leash. He is a hearty eater and an easy keeper as long as he is given a warm place to sleep and fed a nourishing meal. He is friendly and has a high regard for the human race. He is not a yappy dog, as are some breeds. Many of the old-time breeders noted that he does not thrive as a kennel dog, much preferring the companionship of his owners.

The Boston Terrier is the real thing, as Ch. Oui's Hi Stepn Coca Cola Cowboy CD, ROM attests.

Junior handler Sarah Kennedy and some of her winning Bostons—what could be better than a lapful of BTs?

Several big advantages of a Boston are that he is of a nice size, small but not feminine in any way, and he requires a minimum of upkeep. He should have a brushing several times a week to keep his coat clean and glossy and his toenails should be trimmed when needed. Keep his ears cleaned and you may prefer to cut the whiskers with a scissors. If you should be showing your dog, this will be necessary. Cut them as short as possible. An occasional bath, especially during the warm weather months, will also be appreciated by your dog. And these are the basic grooming requirements for the breed.

"An American Gentleman," truly an ideal name for such a fine breed!

Bathing with a friend or five or six keeps life interesting and squeaky clean. Owner, S. Uzoff.

Clowns year 'round, these two elves are Boomer and Fanny, owned by Marilyn Randall.

Spring, summer, fall and winter: the Boston is a dog for all seasons. Enjoying the flowers and scents of spring are Eli, Holly and Jypsie, owned by Susan Herber.

Cooling off in the summertime can make a splash, as demonstrated by the graceful Ch. Oui's Lil Miss Brigitte Bardot.

Autumnal recreation as the leaves fall, here's the very talented Jypsies Jem UD, owned by Susan Herber.

Sweatered from the cold, these Lucky Lady Bostons are helping grandma make an angel in the snow. Owners, Bert and Bertha Zimmerman.

Purchasing Your Boston Terrier

It must be remembered that when you purchase a pet, be it a cat or a dog, the animal will become a part of your family and will probably be with you from 5 to 15. Although you weren't afforded a choice with your own brothers or sisters, when you elect to bring home block; do not bring home a puppy that grows into a 100-pound dog and no longer fits into your two-room apartment. And for Heaven's sake, do not buy the puppy that hangs back in the box because you feel sorry for him. When you add this member to the family, take

Selecting your Boston Terrier from a basketful of well-bred puppies like these from Kap's Bostons should be no problem!

a pet you get to select the one that you think will fit into the family the best and who will be a welcomed addition to your family's style of living.

Buying a dog should require some study and some time. Do not rush out to the pet shop and bring home the dog that looks the neediest; do not run out to your neighbor who breeds her bitch every six months to the male down the a good look at what you are buying and make certain that this is what your family wants and needs.

Consider the purchase of your dog as a major purchase. You may take six months or so to select your new car or a major appliance. Take at least that long to select your dog. You may have the car for five years but your puppy will become a family member for all the years of his life—and that will probably be at least 8 years and may be as much as 12 or 14 years. And, as they say, having a dog is just like having a child, except he never grows up.

Your first step is this one! Read this book cover to cover, and then you'll be on the road to responsible Boston Terrier ownership. The next step that you should take is to attend a local all-breed dog show and watch the Boston Terrier judging. Look over your catalog and see who the breeders are and which kennels the winners are coming from. After the judging, talk to these breeders and ask any questions that you still have in regard to Boston ownership.

The irresistible Kap's Bronco Billy ready for the holidays. Owners, Kent and Jane Peters.

Throughout this book we have referred to "reputable" breeders. A reputable breeder is one who is devoted to making certain that you and the Boston Terrier are suited to each other. He will want to know that you will offer a good home life, including a fenced-in yard and the attention and the love that the dog will need. A reputable breeder has carefully selected his breeding animals and is continually striving to produce better dogs. He has checked the health of his puppies, has wormed them, given them their shots and has done his best not to have bred into any genetic problems. A reputable breeder will sell you a Boston that *looks* like a Boston and has the proper Boston temperament.

A reputable breeder should belong to a local all-breed club, a regional Boston Terrier club and/or the national club (Boston Terrier Club of America). Do not hesitate to ask the breeder to which organizations he belongs, how active he has been and how long he has been a member.

Introducing the litter to little people is an important part of socialization. Ch. Tarbay's Sailing for Glory shares her litter with her young friend. Owner, Marilyn Randall.

Eli, at eight weeks of age, is smelling her first flowers.

season every six months or so, unless you have her spayed. Females seem to mature more quickly than the males and with their first season they quickly become young ladies and lose some of their puppy giggles. Males can remain like a rambunctious teenager for a long time.

Do not have a closed mind to an older dog. Some breeders will have a two or three year old that they would like to place... perhaps the dog has finished its championship and there is no longer a place in the breeder's program for it. Or, perhaps they need to move an older dog on to make room for a promising puppy. There are many advantages to this. The dog is

Ryan Randall, grandson of breeder Marilyn Randall, helps socialize a young pup.

When you visit a kennel, look around and see that it is clean and well cared for. The yard should be clean, the kennel area well lit and the puppies should be fat and happy. They should enjoy seeing a stranger and will not cower in a corner. The breeder should show you the dam of the litter, and if the sire is on the premises, you should meet him too. These dogs should be in good condition with shiny coats and good temperaments.

A reputable breeder may not have a puppy for you when you are ready to buy one. Often breeders only have one or two litters a year and you may have to wait until the next breeding. A reputable breeder will not push a six week old puppy on you but will keep the pup until it is ten or twelve weeks old and ready to leave his nest. Just be patient and the right puppy will come your way.

Give some consideration to whether or not you want a male or a female. A female will come into mature and probably housetrained; if not, it is a quick learner. The mature dog will not chew the rugs and he will be well socialized. Recently we added a four-year-old champion, Group winner to our household and have found him a delight in every way.

If you are a first-time Boston Terrier owner and have never shown a dog, you can expect the breeder to sell you a good dog with a good pedigree, but do not expect that you will receive an animal that will go Best in Show its first time out. It's always possible, of course,

The breeder can assist first-time owners in selecting the Boston Terrier pup that best fits in with his lifestyle and intentions for the dog. Three winners from Anchor Kennels, owned by Norman and Marilyn Randall.

Do not buy your dog from a puppy mill, individuals who may be breeding as many as one hundred dogs of various breeds. You may pay as much for the dog as you would from a reputable breeder and you will probably end up with a dog that doesn't look very much like a Boston Terrier.

just as possible as winning the super lottery, and your chances will be just about the same. For your first dog, you are looking for a pet, a family member . . . and that is just what the breeder will sell you: a well-bred, healthy, well-adjusted Boston Terrier whom your family will enjoy for many years.

Ch. Tarbay's Sailing for Glory with Marilyn Motott, granddaughter of breeder Marilyn Randall.

Two three-month-old babies, the future Ch. Krak-Mont's Final Impression and Ch. Krak-Mont's Final Empress. Owners, Krak-Mont kennels.

Dick and Janet Rees share these four beauties with us: Ch. Bar None's Elegance, Ch. Rees' Amber Elegance, Ch. Rees' Captivating Cameo, and Ch. KimKev's American Classic.

Aust-NZ Ch. Rossdhu Knight Tempera, a specialty and Group winner owned by the Colquohouns of New Zealand.

Ch. Rowdy Dowdy of Romance, owned by Charles Schmidt.

Oui Bostons' first champion, Ch. What's Up Tiger Lily, the dam of Ch. Oui's Hi Stepn Coca Cola Cowboy CD, ROM, owned by S. Maxine Uzoff.

Ch. Bo-K's Spit 'N Polish ROM, owned by Bob and Karen Milham.

Ch. Brandy's Davy Crockett, breeder-owner-handled by Bruce and Sandy Crook.

Ch. Al-Mar's Totallie Awesome ROM (and a great view), owned by Pat Kennedy. Sired by Ch. Al-Mar's Sean O'Tara out of Regal Legacy's Awesome Spell.

Four talented and titled Bostons owned by Kent and Jane Peters: Tucker's Moonbeam CD, Ch. Sabe's Molly McKee, Ch. Kap's Caitlin Shiloh, and Ch. Kap's Keeley Blue Moon.

Hands-on affection makes a Boston Terrier grow up into a confident and social dog. A little love-in underway at the Randalls'.

Christmas is no time for a puppy to arrive. Wrap up a photograph and some dog toys if you're intending on gifting a loved one with a Boston baby for the holiday. The future Ch. Kap's Caitlin Shiloh, bred by Kent and Jane Peters, thanks you on behalf of Bostons everywhere!

Puppies enjoying the cozy life—soft bedding and fun toys—ah, puppyhood!

Ch. Beacon's Do-Go Sunny of Sabe, bred and owned by Ron and Sharon Saberton.

A champion from *Oui* Bostons (that's pronounced "weeeee," so says Ch. Oui's Lil Miss Brigitte Bardot). Owner, S. Maxine Uzoff.

An American original, here's Ch. Jondan's Those Dandy Bubbles, owned by Mr. and Mrs. John Milner.

Daniel Milner, spending time with some of the family Bostons.

The hot summer is no time for Boston Terriers, but don't tell Lil Miss Brigitte Bardot!

Cool water and shade with good friends can make the summer bearable and shareable.

Noel and Dolly, owned by Nancy Lux, show off the photogenic flair!

The holidays can really hang you up the most, so says the nine-week-old future Ch. Oui's First Class Frequent Flyer, owned by S. Maxine Uzoff.

Three capped Kap's pups: Caitlin Shiloh, Barney and Bronco Billy, dressed aptly festive for the holidays.

Ch. Kennedy's C'est La Vie, owned by Vicki Kennedy.

Ouray Two Hearts Forevermore, learning the show stack at 16 weeks of age. Start them early!

No questions asked! Here's a scene from the kitchen of Bert and Bertha Zimmerman. Must have been a long night....

The Boston Terrier is a multi-talented dog, as Ouray's Rumplestiltskin CD attests. He is an excellent hunting dog that specializes in water fowl.

Greetings from the three-month-old Kennedy's Tally Ho, owned by Vicki Kennedy.

The canine family of Gary and Susan Herber, the large yellow Boston Terrier is named Brutus. The family has kept this secret for years: Brutus doesn't know he's a Labrador.

The Boston Terrier in the Show Ring

Dog shows have been in existence in America for well over one-hundred years. Established in 1877, the Westminster Kennel Club dog show, held every year in New York City in early February, is the second oldest annual sporting event in the county with only the Kentucky Derby

becoming an active breeder you will have to be out and about at the shows, either showing your own dogs or having them shown by a professional handler.

I attended my first match show in 1964 with an Old English Sheepdog, encouraged by a friend who showed a

Skilled handlers, whether professionals or owners, show the Boston Terrier off to its best advantage. The handlers must be as well groomed and attentive as their Bostons are.

having greater longevity. In 1917 Ch. Peter's Captain, a Boston Terrier owned by Mrs. George E. Dresser, was Best in Show at this most prestigious of canine events.

Dog shows and dog show competition is not for everyone, but if you are intent on

Great Dane. Four hundred dogs were crammed into a little building. I thought that everyone was crazy, but I was intrigued. Several months later I attended my second show...the Minneapolis Kennel Club's annual all-breed show, which was benched at that time. "This,"

I thought, "is what a dog show is about!" 1500 dogs sitting on benches, wide aisles, breeders and spectators exchanging stories and pedigrees. My third show was in Iowa and I rode with a friend who had recently purchased a St. Bernard. We didn't know about dog crates so my OES rode loose in the rear of the station wagon, the wife and I sat in the midsection and my friend drove, with the Saint sitting next to him on the front seat. The wife traveled the 300-mile trip with a whisk broom in her hand and hit the Saint on the head every time he tried to climb over the seat to go after the OES in the rear. The weather was cold and the show was held in a cow barn. This was not an easy beginning to the sport of showing dogs!

If you are new to the show ring, do attend a few local shows without your

Handler Jayne Palmer has the complete attention of her little showman.

Judging in progress at the Boston Terrier National Specialty in Allentown, Pennsylvania.

dog to see what the game is about. If you are competitive, have the time and the money to compete, and of course, have a good dog, this may be the sport and hobby for you.

Grooming the Boston Terrier for the show ring is relatively simple, compared to heavily coated breeds, such as the Standard Poodle, or the trimmed breeds, like the Scottish Terrier.

The dog must be clean and have well trimmed toenails. The whiskers on the muzzle and eyebrows should be removed with a scissors. Any hairs that detract from a general sleek appearance should be removed with thinning shears. Chalk, talc or other whitener should be rubbed in the white of the coat so that it will be "chalk white." However, do not leave any residue in the coat! Apply a hair tonic, rub it in well and "polish" the coat to make the dark coat glisten. More trimming with a fine thinning shears or a stripping knife can be done wherever you feel that the coat needs to be smoothed out. This is all relatively simple, however it does require some skill and you may not achieve the effects you want on your first try. All the more reason to belong to your local Boston Terrier club where you can get some instructions from an "old pro." Keep working at it and you will achieve what every handler desires with his dog: the look that the dog has never been trimmed at all and was born "perfect!"

If you have not already done so, join your local Boston Terrier club. This is really a must for a novice in the ring. The local club will hold one or two seminars a year that will give you tips on how to show your dog and how to groom your dog for competition. In addition, they will have match shows where you can practice your newly learned skills and have an opportunity to get rid of your

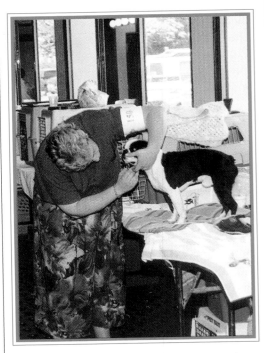

Compared to the other Non-Sporting breeds, the Boston Terrier requires very little in the way of pre-ring preparation. Here a handler is doing some last-minute perfecting before entering the ring.

nervousness. Match shows are run like a dog show, but they are casual and a good place for the beginner to learn. You will not receive any points toward a championship, but you will find out how a dog show is run and you will learn what will be expected of you and your dog. Entry fees at matches are minimal. This is also a good opportunity to meet the people in the breed.

Contact your local all-breed club and find out if they offer conformation classes and start attending these classes on a regular basis. Remember, one class does not an expert make! Your all-breed club will hold one or two matches a year, and you should plan to attend these events. When you think that you are ready, your dog can walk on a lead and you feel a tiny bit of confidence, enter an AKC licensed dog show. Dog shows are divided into seven Groups of dogs of which the Non-Sporting dogs are the sixth Group. The order of the Groups are: Sporting, Hounds, Working, Terrier, Toys, Non-Sporting, and Herding. You will enter your dog as a Boston Terrier and you will enter as either a Dog (male) or a Bitch (female). Unless your dog is a champion, you must enter either the puppy 6- to 12- month Puppy class, the 12- to 18-month class, Novice, American Bred (no imports), Bred by Exhibitor (you are listed as the breeder/owner of the dog) or the Open class. If you are inexperienced, you may want to consider the American Bred class, or the 12- to 18-month old class if your dog is no longer eligible for the puppy class. For Boston Terrier, in the Open class, you will also enter your dog by weight: Open Under 15 pounds, Open 15 pounds and under 20 pounds or Open 20 pounds and not to exceed 25 pounds. Enter your dog in the Open class where the two of you can work as a team and your confidence is in hand.

The judge will place each class first, second, third and fourth. Each class winner of the sex will compete for Winners, i.e., the best dog or bitch of the class (non-champion) dogs. After the non-champion dogs and bitches are judged, the champions of both sexes and the Winners Dog and the Winners Bitch (best of the class dogs and class bitches) will compete for Best of Breed. The judge will then select the Boston Terrier that he feels represents the breed the best for that day. This is the dog that will go into the Group representing the Boston Terrier in the Non-Sporting Group. (Josephine Rine wrote, "Why is the Boston in the Non-Sporting rather than in the terrier Group at the shows? Because, though for life itself he borrowed from the terrier, he actually is no terrier at all and never did a lick of work. A pet he was designed and pet he has remained...he is a bonafide member of the pure-bred leisure class!"

Again, there will be four placements in the Group and the first-place Non-Sporting dog will go into the Best in Show competition. There will be seven dogs in this class, one from each Group. The Best in Show judge will select the dog that he feels is the best dog in the show. Thus, a dog show that started at 8:00 am with 2000 or 3000 dogs will

Show dogs must be trained to tolerate hands-on inspections from strangers, especially when those strangers are the judge.

finish the day with one dog who has remained undefeated and goes Best in Show.

This is basically how a dog show functions. As a newcomer to showing a dog, you will want to work toward a championship for your dog. This may take only three months, but more likely it will take anywhere from six months to two years, depending upon how often you are able to attend shows, and of course, how often you win!

Rowland Johns wrote in 1933: "What good judges cannot resist is a dog who, having a reasonable number of good points, is able to carry himself as if he owned the whole show." Vincent Perry wrote in regard to Ch. Mighty Sweet Regardless, "There is nothing wooden about her stance. She quivers with life and her eyes defy a judge to turn her down. She doesn't miss a thing going on around her. She looks and acts as if the whole thing was a delightful game which she enjoys thoroughly. Which, to be sure, she does."

Remember, participating successfully in showing dogs requires patience, perseverance, time, money, skill and talent. It is the only sport where the amateur and the professional compete on an equal footing. The average dog show competitor remains active for only four to five years. Personal commitments such as children, work, and other hobbies can be a problem to those who want to compete every weekend. More often, the competitor who does not win enough will find his interest in the sport waning. A poorly bred dog, a dog that does not like to show and a handler who will not take the time to learn how to handle well are all deterrents to staying with the sport of dog showing. It is also well

Ch. Al-Mar's By Invitation Only, stacking nicely on lead for his handler.

to remember the advice of Holland Buckley, who wrote in 1913, "If the day goes against you, your selection of shows and judges is sufficiently large to try again. The awards are, after all, only the expression of one man's judgment, and the best of them at times overlook virtues as well as they sometimes miss bad faults."

You should contact a professional handler if you want your dog shown and want a handler who is used to dogs of the brachycephalic breeds, the flat-faced, short nosed dogs. These dogs need extra care during the hot summer months when they are out at the shows.

You will want a professional handler, a handler who is familiar with the care and showing of a Boston Terrier, and above all, you will want a handler who *wins*! The handler will be able to furnish one or two references if you feel that

Boston Terrier specialty shows can draw hundreds of excellent Bostons from around the country. These shows are the ideal place to meet the folk who have a finger on the pulse of the Boston Terrier breed.

are unable to do it yourself, either because of work and time commitments or because you just don't want to enter the ring and compete. A professional handler is an individual whose livelihood is handling dogs and also often boards and grooms dogs. Be sure to inquire about the background of a handler before handing your dog over. You will want one that is familiar with the Boston Terrier, its temperament, and one who is used to working with small dogs that are put on the table for a judge to examine. You will this is necessary. Be sure to inquire as to all costs and find out what will be expected from you as the owner of the dog. In return, the handler will tell you what you can expect from him.

Through the years there have been professional handlers who have been true friends of the Boston Terrier. These are individuals who have shown the great dogs and who have loved the breed. Most have been members of the BTCA and have given freely of their time to help individuals within the breed and

Am-Can. Ch. King Philips Pequoag Drumm'r, owned by Leasa Tyrrell.

the regional breed clubs. Even though they may have shown other breeds, their true love is the Boston Terrier.

In the early years, dog showing was a sport of the wealthy who hired the professionals to handle and condition their dogs. Now, it is the usual to see the owner-handler in the ring, winning top honors with his dogs. The Boston Terrier has had many excellent breeder-owner-handlers who have won the top honors for both their own dogs and for their clients.

Among these dedicated professionals are: Leonard Myers, Marie Ferguson, Norman Randall, Imogene Brown, Harry Clasen, Billie Niegenfeld, Jodi Ghaster Robert Candland Joseph Neibauer Michael Staley and Ann McCammon.

An early *AKC Gazette* columnist wrote about the Boston, "He handles himself like a ballet dancer and is almost as fascinating to watch. For he's about the nearest thing to perpetual motion the dog family can claim...In a show ring he's in his element. He doesn't "ask for his ribbon, " as they say; he positively insists on getting it. For winning or losing, he's a great little showman and knows it." Josephine Rine wrote, "He is clean as a whistle, so short and fine of coat that he cannot hide any part of him. Which should, and probably does, make him the judges' delight—they don't have to poke around under a lot of hair to see what's what!"

And to close, this author wrote the following many years ago, while still owning a few Old English Sheepdogs: "Have you ever been in the ring with your 85 pound dog who's pulling your arm out of the socket while he's trying to lunge out of the gate that he can't see? After getting the situation under

Michael Staley, handling Ch. Maestro's Lucy.

control and while flexing your fingers to see that the circulation is still in them, you look in the next ring where the Toy Poodles are scampering around and you think, "How nice it must be!." Several weeks ago I showed two Scottish Terriers and found out just how nice it is. During the first class I spent most of the time trying to *find* the little fellow—and

Norman Randall, handling Ch. Tarbay's Sailing for Glory, winning WB at the 1991 Centenary Show under breeder-judge Leonard Myers. Trophy presenter, Al Nicks.

then wondered what do with his tail...TAIL! By the time the ten-month-old female and I made the rounds, I learned that you have to get down to their level to work. Consequently I finished that class with a couple of gaping holes around the region of the kneecaps. After I left the ring I surveyed the ridges in my knees from the mats and my by now baggy, laddered panty hose. Throughout it all though, my left arm remained in its socket and the dog did know where it was going every minute of the day...and that was usually after the dog next to her! So, advantages and disadvantages to showing both small and large breeds." I became more proficient in showing the Scottish Terriers and have always maintained that it takes strength to show a

large breed and intelligence to show a small one. The second moral to this story is that you can start your show career not having an inkling of what you are to do, and through time and practice, you can become quite accomplished!"

Michael Staley, breeder-owner-handler, with Ch. Staley's Flashdancer winning the Breed under breeder-judge Colleen Brossard.

117

Ch. Al-Mar's By Invitation Only, bred and owned by Sue and Pat Kennedy, winning the BTCA Centenary show in 1993 under breeder-judge Blanche Leahy. Handler, Sue Kennedy. Sired by Ch. Maestro's Special Whiz out of Ch. Al-Mar's Irish Escapade.

Ch. O.J.s Justamere Rainbow's End, bred by OlaJeanne McCollough and owned by Joanne Hearst and Ann McCammon, winning under breeder-judge Edna Swift.

Ch. PBN Earl's Serenade, the first champion for breeders Brad and Pauline Nedeau, owned by Tom and Joyce Davis.

Ch. Maximillian's Sneak Preview, owned by Brad and Pauline Nedeau.

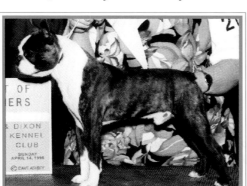

Ch. Krak-Mont's Final Impression, bred and owned by Elizabeth Montgomery.

Ch. Juwell's Lady Annabelle Rose CD, bred and owned by Judy Criswell.

Ch. Staley's Jr's Supercharger, owned by Michael and Beverly Staley.

Ch. Krak-Mont D.J., bred and owned by Elizabeth Montgomery.

Ch. Rees' Classic American Dandy, bred and owned by Richard and Janet Rees. Sired by Ch. Rees' Primetime Classic Cheers out of Ch. Vanity Fair Elegance.

Ch. Rees' Classic American Hero, littermate to Dandy, bred and owned by Richard and Janet Rees. Sired by Ch. Rees' Primetime Classic Cheers out of Ch. Vanity Fair Elegance.

Littermates at their first show, Ch. Kennedy's Sisco's Slam Dunk owned by Dana Sisco, and Kennedy's Knoty Victoria Rose, owned by Leasa Tyrrell.

Ch. KimKev's Nanette, owned by Ed and Susan Adams.

Can. Ch. Abacab's Bold Mischief Encore ROM, breeder-owned by Robin Cameron and Peter Hicks, the dam of at least five American and eight Canadian champions. Sired by Ch. Top Shelf Sweet Lou out of Am-Can. Ch. Bold Mischief at Tijuana.

Ch. Fourstar's Taylors Tom Son, owner-handled by Jayne Palmer, a top-ten Boston in 1996.

Am-Can. Ch. Bold Mischief at Tijuana, an all-breed BIS winner and multiple Group and specialty winner. Owned by Robin Cameron and Peter Hicks and bred by Judy Campbell, she was the number-one Boston in Canada in 1988. Sired by Can. Ch. Tijuana's Bold as Brass CDX out of Can. Ch. Tijuana's Tequila Sunrise.

Kevin Kennedy claims the best junior handler award at the Minuteman BT Club with his dog Ch. Brandy's Kennedy Rudolf Valntno.

Winning sibling junior handlers, Kevin and Sarah Kennedy with their dogs Am-Can. Ch. Kennedy's Storm Watch Bramley and Kennedy's Crown Jewel Bijou.

Junior handler Shannon Criswell with Ch. Juwell's Lady Annabelle Rose CD, winning at the Cheyenne KC.

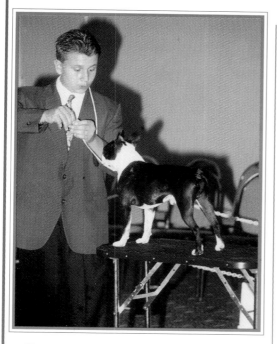

Kevin Kennedy, baiting Rudolf Valntno on the table.

Sarah Kennedy with Kennedy's Crown Jewel Bijou taking home an Award of Merit.

A junior looking like a pro, here's Kevin Kennedy with Ch. Kennedy's Boston Pops.

Breeding Your Boston Terrier

Several thoughts should be kept in mind when you consider breeding your Boston Terrier.

1. Not every bitch needs to be bred. Take a look at your local humane society and see the numbers of unwanted dogs that will eventually be put down for lack of a home.

2. Do not breed your bitch because you want your children to see "Mother Nature at work." There are good videos that can answer their questions.

3. Do not breed your bitch because you want to "make some money." It's just about impossible to make any money on a litter and, in general, it will be a losing operation.

4. Do not breed your bitch because you think "one litter will be good for her." Is a woman "better" because she goes through childbirth?

Think about the following before having a litter of puppies:

1. A litter of puppies is very time consuming. You and the rest of the family will be spending hours with the puppies, cleaning them, worrying over them and socializing them.

Breeding requires not only commitment and knowledge but also money and time. Before considering breeding your Boston Terrier, evaluate your circumstances and goals carefully. Puppies bred by Mr. and Mrs. George Wojtyna.

A litter of four future champions at seven weeks of age, sired by Am-Can. Ch. Top Shelf Crackerjack out of Can. Ch. Abacab's Bold Mischief Encore. Bred by Robin Cameron and Peter Hicks.

2. A litter of puppies is very hard on the house. Rugs are not only soiled but they are often chewed around the corners, as well as the woodwork and furniture chewed. Once outside, the pups can create havoc in the yard.

3. A litter of puppies will cost you money. First, you have a stud fee. Then, your bitch has a great possibility of requiring a caesarian section, which is a substantial expense.

Your puppies will require shots, a large expense if you have a large litter.

4. You can't count on selling your puppies quickly. You may have one or two pups with you until six months of age or more. In the meantime, the family becomes attached to them, your dog food bills continues to rise and your patience runs thin.

If you do decide to breed, answer the following questions:

1. Is your bitch of quality? Does she have a good pedigree, linebred with a championship background? (One champion out of 64 descendants does not make a championship background.)

2. Did you talk to the breeder that you bought your bitch from in regard to breeding her? Did he tell you that you should breed your girl or did he sell her to you as a pet?

3. What stud dog should you breed to? Ask your breeder for his opinion. Use a dog that has a solid pedigree....not only a championship background, but he is a champion and possibly a Group or Best in Show winner. The stud fee for a great dogwill not be much more than for a mediocre dog.

4. When should you have this litter? Spring and summer litters are easier than fall and winter litters as you can have the puppies outside more. Do you

have a big vacation planned for the summer? Is there already a glut of Boston puppies in your area? Ask the reputable breeder, the one with the stud dog that is being used, and she can tell you.

A note in regard to the reputable, experienced breeders: These are the individuals who have been breeding Boston Terriers for ten, twenty or more years. They belong to an all-breed club and to the BTCA. They show their dogs, attend the national shows and keep abreast of the trends in the breed. A wise newcomer will build upon their experience. Don't think that you can come along and breed a "star" with a pet-quality bitch. This happens about as often as winning that lottery. And remember, always start with a quality bitch. You probably won't live long enough to breed up to the quality of the

A breeder's commitment to the breed as well as her rapport with her dogs should be obvious and beaming! Sue Milner showing off her handiwork.

big winners of the day unless you start with quality.

You have decided that you have the quality bitch that should be bred and you are going ahead with this project. You have talked to the breeder of your bitch and it's determined that you should breed her. You have found a good stud dog and you are ready to get to work.

A Boston Terrier bitch will come into season the first time when she is around eight to ten months old and then she will come into season approximately every six months after that. Do not breed your bitch the first season. Wait until she is around eighteen months old and then consider breeding her.

You should contact the owner of the stud dog that you have selected when you first notice that your bitch is in season. You will be told when to bring her, or when to ship her, to the kennels so that she can be bred somewhere between the 11th and 15th days of her esterus.

Your girl has now been bred and by the sixth week of gestation (gestation for dogs is 63 days), you should know if she is pregnant. Decide which room will be the nursery, making sure that you have picked a quiet spot out of the hub-bub of daily living. Sometimes you can borrow a whelping box from another breeder, otherwise a box can be easily made. A wooden box is nice, a wire kennel can be excellent, and a cardboard box is acceptable. The pen should be about 3' by 3' and about 8 to 12 inches high. A guard rail (also called a "pig rail") should be placed around the inside of the box, approximately 3 inches above the ground. This gives the puppies an area to crawl under for protection against the mother's weight when she leans against the side of the box.

If you anticipate a Caesarean section, talk to your veterinarian and the two of you can set up an approximate appointment for the surgery, based upon the dates that she was bred. Start taking her temperature with a rectal thermometer about the 59th days after the first breeding. A dog's temperature averages about 101.5 degrees and as the whelping becomes more eminent the temperature will start to drop. When it settles down to 98 degrees or so, you should be expecting pups within 24 hours. During these days you will also note a sticky and smelly discharge from the vulva, and by now your girl should be quite heavy and may need assistance with the steps. Hold her on your lap and you can feel the puppies moving around! Remember, if you expect a Caesarean, you must keep your veterinarian informed as to her progress and you must follow his instructions for when

Socialization—that is introducing the pups to life experiences—ranks high on the breeder's priority list. These young children are becoming acquainted with two Boston toddlers bred by Marilyn Randall.

All in the family: dam, sire and offspring. Ch. Kennedy's C'est la Vie, Am-Can. Ch. Brandy's Kennedy Rudolf Valntno, and Am-Can. Ch. Kennedy's Storm Watch Bramley. Owners, Kevin and Vicki Kennedy and Ann Lord.

you should bring her in to the clinic.

You can expect between two and four puppies in your litter. Puppies delivered naturally will usually be delivered anywhere from 20 minutes to 3-hour intervals. It's a good idea when the first puppy is delivered to note the time of day, sex and color of the puppy on a note pad. If you

A soon-to-be Boston mom scratching about to make a "nest."

should have a long delay between births, you will have specific information to give your veterinarian if you need to call for assistance.

Puppies are born in a sac and they are attached to the sac by the umbilical cord. Do not break this sac as the pup is emerging from the birth canal. Have patience as it can take up to ten minutes before the pup in the sac "pops" out. When the pup comes out, mother should reach around, open the sac and snip off the umbilical cord with her teeth. At this point, however, many breeders take matters into their own hands and will cut and tie the umbilical cord with a clean scissors, about two inches from the tummy. Again, most breeders, at this point, help the mother by rubbing the puppy dry with a clean terry cloth towel and they will continue to do this until they hear a good, healthy cry from the pup. While doing this, look the puppy over and make sure that everything appears to be in order. Now, you are ready to hand this fellow over to mother and she will wash it all over again and pull the pup up to her nipples.

Puppies and bitch should be kept in a draft-free warm area. Take the mother outside after the whelping is completed and let her relieve herself. Clean up her rear end, put down clean towels or rugs in your box, and make her a dish of

Mom is straining with a really hard contraction.

soft food. Give this to her along with a pan of water.

If you should have a Caesarean section, your veterinarian will be doing all of the work. If you are able to watch as he performs this operation, do, as you will find it very interesting. I have watched many a C-section (and cleaned up a lot

The puppy is emerging, in the breech position.

of puppies) and I still marvel each time I see this operation, at what God and Mother Nature can do!

Note that many Boston litters are by Caesarean section. One Boston breeder wrote that with a free-whelp litter you risk losing puppies but that she also lost as many puppies with a Caesarean section. Therefore, she felt it was a tossup and you have to use your instinct to decide if you should let your bitch free whelp or if she should have a Caesarean. There are several other factors that should be involved in addition to your instinct. If you have a small bitch, you will probably want to consider having a section; if your bitch's dam and granddam had to have sections, your bitch will also probably need one; if your bitch comes from a line of free-whelpers, you can probably let her free whelp. You may also want to discuss this with your veterinarian.

Caesarean puppies are usually pretty pups as they have not had the trauma of working their way down the birth canal. The mother may be a bit slow for the first 24 hours because of the anesthesia, but after that she will be the perfect little mother. You will find it necessary, however, to watch her incision each day, cleaning it with a damp cloth and making sure that it does not become infected.

Bitch has moved attempting to find an easier position to pass the puppy.

The bitch has delivered the puppy, including its sac and placenta.

Mom is licking and cleaning the puppy. She must also remove the sac and bite the cord to sever it.

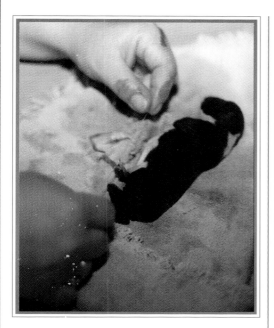

The breeder is tying off the umbilical cord using plain waxed dental floss.

Breeder is holding the puppy in a towel and bracing the back of its neck with her thumbs and front with her fingers. She proceeds to shake the pup down by raising her hands above her head and swinging them between her legs to clear the pup's lungs. This usually takes about three good tries.

The breeder is cutting the cord with a scissors. Hopefully the pup doesn't try to crawl away as this one is doing.

Three-week time lapse: here's two healthy males, eyes open and crawling about.

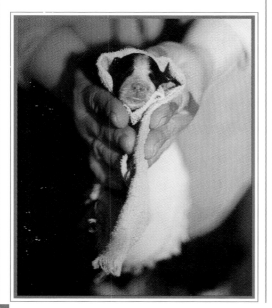

A ready-to-deliver Boston Terrier dam. This series of photographs depicting a Caesarean section courtesy of Kap's Bostons of Kent and Jane Peters.

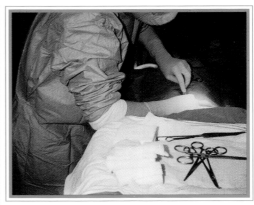

...and makes an incision.

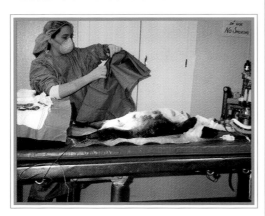

The dam has been tranquilized and put on oxygen. The surgical assistant proceeds with a thorough pre-op scrub down and placing a sterile cloth over the dam.

The veterinarian sterilizes the abdominal area...

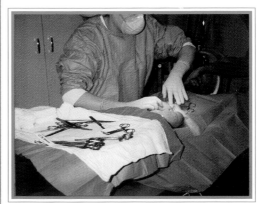

The uterus of the dam is being pulled out.

The uterine horn contains the individual sacs holding each puppy.

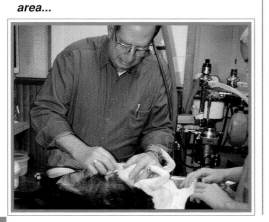

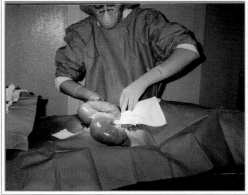

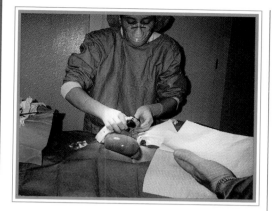

The first puppy has been removed from its sac.

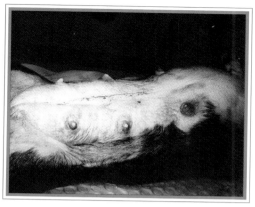

The dam's incision is sutured.

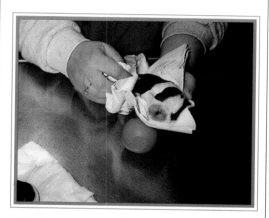

Each puppy must be cleaned ....

Three healthy puppies being kept warm.

...and its umbilical cord severed.

The dam has recovered from her surgery and the puppies are nursing contentedly.

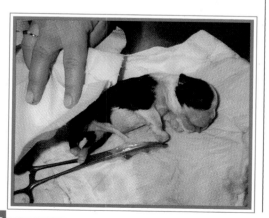

RAISING A HEALTHY LITTER

Your litter has now been whelped and the first five days of your puppies' lives are their most important ones.

You can do some simple things to help ensure healthy puppies: keep the whelping box and the puppies in a draft-free area; keep the

Litter bred by Vernon and Kristie Wheeler, being kept warm by a heating pad. These babies are under two weeks of age.

temperature in the whelping room at a minimum of 75 degrees; see that your dam is staying healthy, eating well, and drinking water.

This is what you want to see when you look in your whelping box: A contented mother and a contented litter. The puppies should be tucked up around her, alternately sleeping and nursing. They should be quiet, happy and warm.

Watch for the following trouble signs: body temperature drop, no weight gain, dehydration. Check for dehydration by pinching the skin. On a healthy pup, the skin pops back into place; on a dehydrated pup the skin stays pinched. If your dam appears listless or if your whole litter starts crying, you have a problem. Call your veterinarian and tell him that you are bringing your bitch in and ask him if he also wants to see the puppies.

Remember this when raising a litter: most litters are healthy litters. Your puppies will usually survive and your mothers will usually be attentive and healthy.

At just 11 days of age, two males and three females bred by Brandy Bostons of Bruce and Sandy Crook.

Zuran's Kibbles & Bits, sleeping comfortably with her puppies. Owners, Vernon and Kristie Wheeler.

You should do whatever you can to ensure that the above takes place. Keep your whelping pen clean, an easy job for the first two weeks or so, as the mother does most of the work. Feed the mother properly. If it is a large litter, you will probably have to increase her food, feeding her several times a day when the pups are approximately three weeks old. Look over each puppy every day and make sure that everything is functioning.

A short aside about dying pups: pups do die, no matter how you might try and save them. Here is a general rule of thumb: a cold puppy is a dead puppy. A puppy that the mother persistently ignores and pushes to the side of the pen will usually be a dead puppy within a matter of hours. Something is wrong with the pup and the mother and knows it.

Use your discretion about how much you want to do to save this kind of puppy.

Let's assume that all is going well and that your litter is bopping along, getting fat and looking happy. Remember Bostons are slow in maturing compared to some breeds. Their eyes will open in 10 to 12 days but they will be 2 to 3 weeks of age before they are on their feet and not until 3 weeks of age will they develop curiosity and move about. Don't worry and let them develop at their own pace.

Start weaning your litter at three to four weeks. The larger the litter, the more important it is to start weaning early to help mother with the feeding.

When you start to wean your puppies, mix up a gruel of high-quality puppy kibble. Make a very mushy meal with no lumps in it. At the time you start to feed your pups, offer them a pan of water also. Bostons, probably due to an elongated soft palate, at first, usually need a much wetter weaning formula than other breeds do because they can choke easier and may aspirate kibble

An active litter ready to explore the world.

leave him looking like a smart Boston. A poor ear trim can leave your puppy looking like a Miniature Schnauzer or a Great Dane!

By now you should have trimmed the puppies toenails several times. It is now time to start setting up each puppy on the grooming table and wiping the puppy down with a damp cloth. Select a grooming table with an arm and a noose for maximum security and efficiency. It is never too early to get them used to being handled and used to being groomed. Be sure to put the dog's head in the noose for control while grooming and do not leave him unattended at any time.

Decide how long you want to keep your pups before placing them in a home. A pup really should never go to a new home before 8 weeks of age and many breeders like to keep them until

At just seven weeks old, Oui's Whoopsie Daisy is getting a feel for the grass.

into their lungs. As the pups start to eat more on their own and as their teeth start to come in, your mother will become less and less interested in spending time with the pups.

When your puppies are five to six weeks old, take them to your veterinarian for their shots. Your vet will tell you which shots they should have and how many times they need to be repeated. At this time, you should also take in a stool sample for analysis. If your pups are wormy, your veterinarian will give you the proper medication to clear up the worms. (One stool sample from one pup is sufficient for this analysis.)

Ear trimming is strictly a matter of choice today and not done as much as it once was. Ears are not trimmed until the head has reached maturity, somewhere between six to ten months. Select a veterinarian who is familiar with Boston ears so that your Boston will receive an ear trim that will

Can. Ch. Ouray Two Hearts Teddy Bear Am-Can. CD with four-week-old son, Bruno. Owners, Ouray Bostons.

12 weeks. When the pup goes to its new home, have it clean and smelling good! Give the new owner a list of the food that is being used and note the number of times a day that you are feeding. Give him the name of a veterinarian in his area. It's nice to add one of the little Boston breed books and a leash too. Of course, send the registration papers and a copy of the pedigree.

With your first litter it may be hard to see the rascals go off to a new home. However, keep in mind that it is rather nice to have one of these little bundles that you have spent so much time on go off into its own little world and be appreciated and loved by others.

E. B. White wrote, "My Christmas will be a whole lot wetter and merrier,

If somebody sends me a six-weeks old Boston terrier."

The future Ch. Chasen Kennedy's I Heard A Rumor at seven weeks of age, owned by Kip and Vicki Kennedy.

The future Ch. Kap's Caitlin Shiloh, bred by Kent and Jane Peters.

Four-week-old litter owned by Kip and Vicki Kennedy.

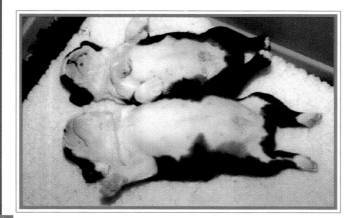

Sound asleep at four weeks, these two dolls are Oui Bostons.

Dolly, owned by Nancy Lux, doesn't know that she's not a "real" terrier.

A heartfelt hello from two Boston tikes, owned by Lucinda McIntosh.

Growing fast at seven weeks, this litter was bred by Susan Greene.

A foster-mom Rottweiler raised this litter of Boston Terrier pups. Photograph courtesy of Leasa Tyrrell.

At nine weeks of age, future Ch. Oui's First Class Frequent Flyer, owned by Oui Bostons.

Female Boston at four weeks of age, bred by Brandy Bostons.

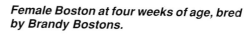

Am-Can. Ch. Top Shelf Crackerjack ROM is the celebrated sire of several Group and specialty winners. Owned by Robin Cameron and Peter Hicks and bred by Tom and Suzanne Ghaster, Willy was sired by Am-Can. Ch. Ri-Ja's Bronco Billy out of Ch. Top Shelf Starwitness.

Am-Can. Ch. Abacab's Midnite Madness, bred and owned by Robin Cameron and Peter Hicks, won two all-breed best puppy awards and went on to win multiple Group firsts. Dixie was sired by Am-Can. Ch. Top Shelf Crackerjack ROM out of Can. Ch. Abacab's Bold Mischief Encore ROM.

Am-Can. Ch. Abacab's Total Eclipse, bred and owned by Robin Cameron and Peter Hicks, won the Canadian National and multiple Group firsts. Teddy was sired by Am-Can. Ch. Top Shelf Crackerjack ROM out of Can. Ch. Abacab's Bold Mischief Encore ROM.

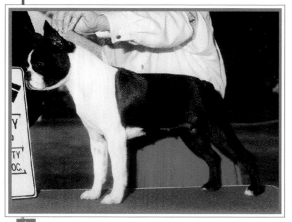

Ch. Oui's Hi Stepn Coca Cola Cowboy UD, ROM, owner-breeder-handled by S. Maxine Uzoff, was the sire of number-one Boston bitch in 1990 and again in 1995. Judge, Emil Klinckhardt.

Ch. WC's Victoria's Secret of Oui, number-one bitch and number-two Boston in 1995, sired by Ch. Oui's Hi Stepn Coca Cola Cowboy UD, ROM, owner-bred by S. Maxine Uzoff.

Ch. CG's Hi Stepn Oui Tambourine, sired by Ch. Oui's Hi Stepn Coca Cola Cowboy UD, ROM, owned by Gary and Carol Moore.

Ch. KimKev's Buchanen, owned by Robert Breum and handled by Al Lee. Sired by Zodiac's Special Beau out of Ch. Showman's Lovely Debbie.

Ch. KimKev's American Classic, owned by Richard and Janet Rees and bred by Betty Swick. Sired by Ch. Zodiac's Special Beau out of Ch. Showman's Lovely Debbie.

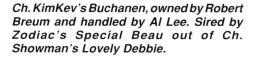

All of the following dogs were bred by Betty Swick. Sire: Ch. Zodiac's Special Beau. Dam: Ch. Showman's Lovely Debbie.

Am-Can. Ch. KimKev's All American Girl, breeder-owned by Betty Swick. Sired by Ch. Zodiac's Special Beau out of Ch. Showman's Lovely Debbie.

Am-Can. Ch. KimKev's Kalamity Jane, breeder-owned by Betty Swick. Sired by Ch. Zodiac's Special Beau out of Ch. Showman's Lovely Debbie.

Ch. Tiz Sam's Kidd O'Sage'N Sand, bred Bud and Norma Howell, owned by Florence Brooks. Sired by Ch. Howell's Sage'N Sand Tuxedoman out of Madame Beulah's Little Lady.

Ch. Kidd's Dandy Boy Beau, breeder-owned by Florence Brooks. Sired by 'Tiz Sam's Kidd O'Sage'N Sand out of Sage'N Sand Kaptain's Kibbles.

Ch. Kaptain's Whiz Kid, breeder-owned by Florence Brooks. Sired by Am-Can. Ch. Sage'N Sand Kaptain Kidd out of Mary's Little Whiz.

Ch. Sage'N Sand Kaptain Kidd's Jr, breeder-owned by Florence Brooks. Sired by Am-Can. Ch. Sage'N Sand Kaptain Kidd out of Sage'N Sand Shea-Dee Lady.

Am-Can. Ch. Sage'N Sand Kaptain Kidd, owned by Florence Brooks. Sired by Ch. 'Tiz Sam's Kidd O'Sage'N Sand out of Mazie's Sage'N Sand Surprise.

The Health of Your Boston Terrier

By and large, the Boston Terrier is considered to be a healthy breed, with no more genetic problems or health problems than most other breeds. Give your Boston care, use your common sense and have a good veterinarian available. Find a reliable veterinarian who is familiar with the brachycephalic breeds. Find a vet that you trust, take your dog in when you think that you have a problem, follow instructions and recovery will usually be very rapid.

The short-nosed Boston Terrier requires special consideration in very hot or very cold climates. This kissable Boston is owned by Vicki Kennedy.

Your dog should have yearly inoculations along with a stool sample run to make certain that he is free from worms. Keep the teeth clean and the nails trimmed. Your veterinarian can do these jobs if you or your groomer are unable to do so. Watch for ticks in the summer and any wounds should be cleaned out. Some wounds may require veterinary care. Yearly heartworm checks in some areas of the country are also important.

If your veterinarian is not available at odd hours for emergencies, know where the emergency veterinarian is located and keep his telephone number handy. Many veterinarians in large cities no longer have an emergency service and you must rely on these special facilities for late evening, weekend and holiday service.

Keep your dog groomed and clean. Watch the ears for ear mites or other infections. For Bostons it is very important to keep them out of the sun in the summer and certainly don't ever leave him in the car on a hot day. Likewise, in the winter, with their short coats, it is wise to have a jacket for them when they go outside. Because of their "pushed-in nose" the Bostons, as do French Bulldogs, English Bulldogs, and other similar breeds, do not tolerate the heat and cold as well as long-nosed breeds.

Your dog should be kept in either a fenced yard or on a leash. It's foolish, and often against the

The picture of good health and vigor, the well-bred Boston Terrier is a purebred that has relatively few serious health concerns. This healthy lady is owned by Leasa Tyrrell.

law, to let your dog run loose and take a chance of him being run over by a car. Too often the story is heard about the dog that lives at the end of the cul-de-sac where only one delivery truck comes along a day, and that truck runs over the dog. It only takes one vehicle to end a dog's life.

Dogs often live to seven or eight years and then die of some disease. It seems that if your Boston lives to eight years of age, your chances are good that you will have another two to six years with him. Eleven and twelve year old Bostons are not unusual. Remember, anything after eight years, in any breed, is considered to be a gift.

The Boston is a brachycephalic breed and congenital problems are primarily because of this. Cleft palates, hare lips and edematous (walrus) puppies are not uncommon. An edematous puppy is obvious at birth as this will be a very large, water-filled puppy. These puppies will die Many years ago I had friends who raised champion Bulldogs and they told a pediatric surgeon about this problem. The surgeon decided he could solve this problem and the next time a litter was expected, the bitch in whelp, her owners, two physicians and a lot of equipment made the trek to the veterinarian's clinic—owned by an excellent, old-time vet who had been around for years. After considerable work, the two "water babies" died and the vet later told me, "Oh, I could have told them from the very beginning that the puppies would die, but the doctors were so persistent and sure that they could save these puppies that I didn't want to disappoint them."

The breeder who screens his lines for eye problems will have healthy, alert puppies. Owner, Marilyn Randall.

A brother-sister combo from Kap's Bostons, owned by Kent and Jane Peters. This is Kap's Wild Rose Jessie and future Ch. Kap's Beau by Sunny.

Again, puppies with cleft palates should be put down immediately as they cannot survive as they are unable to nurse. Be sure to check the palates of all of your puppies to see if there is a problem.

Juvenile cataracts is a hereditary problem and is a very serious genetic disorder in the Boston Terrier, as well as in several other breeds. In the Boston Terrier it is always bilateral and the two eyes are very similar in appearance. Diagnosis can be made as early as eight weeks of age. At this time, suture lines will appear as fine dark lines but changes become more obvious and by four months of age, with direct light, a faint opaque, triangular area is visible in the pupil. At six months of age, a slit-lamp examination shows that the cataract involves most of the lens. This is a hereditary problem: breeders must be diligent in their breeding and not breed dogs, or breed to dogs, that are infected or are known carriers. You can ask the breeder of your puppy if she has an eye certification for her dogs stating that they are clear of juvenile cataracts.

GERIATRIC BOSTONS

The geriatric dog, those over eight years of age, may require a little more or different care than the younger dog. As your dog ages, he will slow down and possibly have some arthritis. His sight and hearing starts waning and he may sleep more. Let him have his ways. Do not expect him to do the three-mile walk as he did as a pup. You may want to try dog food for the geriatric or sedate dog. Be sure he has a warm space to sleep and try to keep him at a normal weight as excess weight can be difficult on the rheumatoid bones.

As he ages and becomes more infirm, you will eventually be forced with the decision of "putting your dog down." Unfortunately, dogs and humans do not die very often in their sleep. With the dog we are able to make a decision

JoshNJyps Jalepeno Pepper CD, TDI, aka Holly, owned by Gary and Susan Herber.

of being a humane owner, and the day may come when you take your pet in to be euthanized by your veterinarian. It's hard to know when "it's time" but again, use your common sense and try not to let your dog suffer unduly. Your veterinarian will administer a very quick drug and you will be surprised how quickly and peacefully he will die in your arms. This is a terribly sad day for the entire family but it often takes only a few weeks, or months, before you are looking for your new Boston Terrier.

Eli, Jypsie, and Holly, owned by Gary and Susan Herber.

Working With Your Boston Terrier

Every Boston Terrier should be able to lie around the house, have a good meal, receive love and attention and be taken for a walk or a romp every day. However, some owners like the challenge, bonding and companionship of working with their dog and of training him to follow commands.

OBEDIENCE

For obedience work, dog *and* handler need aptitude and determination. The handler must take time to work his dog every day, even if it is only for five minutes or so. The handler must also have patience and the dog must have a desire to perform and at least some willingness to please. Fortunately, Bostons have a temperament and a natural willingness to please and this will make your job easier than it would be if you had a fairly stubborn dog. Once this match is made, a handler and his dog can be well on their way toward the obedience degrees. The handler will feel a tremendous amount of achievement and accomplishment to have such a smart little dog working by his side. Spectators at a dog show love to watch the obedience rings as they can understand what the dog is doing (or not doing) much better than when they watch the conformation rings. There is no better sight than watching the Boston, in his "bib and tucker," flying over the hurdles."

Sara Casey's Connemara's Kitty O'Shea UD, flying over the hurdles at an obedience trial.

Obedience classes are offered throughout the country and unless you live in a very remote area, your town or city should offer you a selection of training opportunities. Some classes are offered by private individuals, others offered by obedience clubs or all-breed clubs. There are different methods of instruction and you may find it worthwhile to visit various classes to see which method of training you prefer.

You will usually start your pup at about six months of age, and some classes will not take a dog any younger. Classes will meet once or twice a week for six to ten weeks. Having successfully completed one of these classes, and successful means passing the examination at the end of the class, you should have a dog that will sit on command, come when called and will walk decently on a lead. This is all that many dog owners require. They want a pet that behaves like a gentleman or a lady. If you have never owned a dog before, or never owned a dog with good manners, obedience class work may be just what you want and need.

For those who have a genuine interest in obedience, your classwork will continue beyond this and you will start working for degrees and titles, just as you would with a dog in the conformation ring. At this point, if you have not been training with an obedience club, you may want to consider finding one that you can join.

The American Kennel Club offers the following obedience titles: Companion Dog (CD) is earned in Novice class, Companion Dog Excellent (CDX) is earned in Open class and a Utility Dog (UD) degree is earned in the Utility class.

To earn a degree, the dog must qualify for at least 170 of the 200 points at a trial and you must win half of the points

Halsey Fredericks with Molly, a rescue Boston Terrier. Exactly one year from the day she entered the Fredericks' home, she earned her CDX, to become number two in obedience.

in each exercise. When a dog has qualified, he has earned a "leg." Three legs under three different judges must be earned before the dog receives his title. Once a title is earned, it becomes a part of the dog's name, just as Ch. (Champion) becomes a part of the name when won in the conformation ring. Except for the Obedience Trial Champion (OTCh.), obedience titles are added at the end of the name rather than at the beginning.

In an obedience trial you are competing against yourself. If there are 20 in the class and 10 receive scores of 170 or more, ten dogs will receive their leg at that show. In conformation showing, you compete against all other dogs as there is only one Best of Breed dog.

Novice classes consist of heeling on lead, standing for examination, coming when called and the long sit (one minute), and the long down (three minutes). In Open classes all work is done off lead, which includes heeling, coming when called, dropping to a down position on command, retrieving a dumbbell and jumping over the broad jump. In Utility the exercises become much more complicated and

are offered in your area. A match is an opportunity for you to work your dog in a show-like setting without paying the fee required for entering an AKC-licensed obedience trial. Entry fees for a match are minimal and judging will be done by amateurs who have done considerable obedience work. You cannot earn any "legs" at a match, but you will learn how a show works and what will be required of you and your dog.

Ch. Anchor's Special Jazz winning at the BTCA 1994 National with owner Dorothy Truman.

include signals, scent exercises, directed retrieve, and directed jumping. As can be seen, these are ambitious programs requiring great effort and patience on both the handler's and the dog's part.

If you decide to work toward an obedience degree, lessons and class work are just about essential. Daily practice is also a must. If you become active in an obedience club you will be aware of the obedience matches that

The Utility Dog Excellent (UDX) title went into effect in January 1994. It requires qualifying simultaneously ten times in Open B and Utility B but not necessarily at consecutive shows.

Boston Terriers have been active in obedience work for decades and a well-trained Boston is always welcomed in nursing homes, senior citizen homes and schools to put on a good display of obedience work for the crowd. Everyone loves to watch a dapper little dog who will

Jypsies Jim UDX, Can. CD, TDI, owned by Gary and Susan Herber, winning at the BTCA 1995 National under judge Judith A. Brown.

Jypsies Jem, UDX, NA, Can. CD, TD is now working toward her Novice Agility Dog degree as well as her Canadian CDX. Nancy Ames' Sweet Sociable Samuel was the first Boston to earn the AKC Agility title and also the first to win a NAFA Flyball dog title (1990). Sara Casey's Connemara's Kitty O'Shea, UD, was the only Boston to earn a UD between November 1993 and April 1996. She was among the top ten obedience Bostons in the early 1990s.

come on call, retrieve an object with a hand signal, and jump over a hurdle, all completed with a zest-for-life attitude! The BTCA offers several annual trophies for obedience work.

Some exceptional winning Bostons in obedience have been OTCh. Brother Mack Duff, owned by Ellen Dresselhuis—the first Boston *ever* to win an OTCH. When Mac completed his Obedience Trial Championship he not only won the utility class, putting him several points over the 100 required for the OTCh., but he also won his Open class with a score of 199 points out of 200. He was tied with two other dogs and won the run-off. Therefore, that day he was high in trial and high combined score in Open and Utility. Quite an accomp-lishment! Sue Herber's

Elizabeth Wieland, from Kentucky, wrote about her Dynamite Dixie Darlin, "She has given me a lot of confidence in training and showing, but the best thing about her is she is my buddy. She is always ready for a walk, ride, game of fetch, 'Boston soccer' or anything else we might want to do."

Pauline Nedeau wrote about her Ch. Maximillian's Sneak Preview, CD, "He is

Taking a break from the competition at an obedience trial. Here's Boston Terrier Doc with German Shepherd comrade, Tasha. Owner, Brandy Bostons.

also a therapy dog, and loves to dress up in costumes. He has won Best Kisser and Best Costume at the State Fair in the Upper Peninsula of Michigan. Last, but not least, he is my pride and joy and my best friend!"

Eleanor Jackson from Pennsylvania has shown three Bostons in obedience trials, beginning in 1968. Her bitch, Jackson's Jeanie Garrett finished her CDX in 1973 and at that time Eleanor was notified that this was the 133rd Boston in obedience history to earn the CDX title. Another of their dogs, Jackson's Spunky Punkin earned her UD title in 1982 with high qualifying scores. The third Boston, Jackson's Bouncing Bittyboo, finished her UD in 1993. All three dogs completed their obedience degrees with high scores, consistently placing among

Pauline Nedeau with Ch. Maximillians Sneak Preview CD, taking a first place.

Elizabeth Wieland with Dynamite Dixie Darlin, winning a first place.

the top obedience Bostons in the country. Eleanor wrote, "They all have made me very happy and I am proud of their records." As well she should be!

Trophie Frederick of Pennsylvania owned Trophie's Incredible Cricket, a triple Utility degree Boston. In September 1977, *Front and Finish* magazine wrote about Cricket and the speed with which she completed her obedience degrees: "her eagerness to please had always characterized this 10 pound sweetie." Trophie has trained and shown numerous Bostons to their international titles (American, Canadian and Bermudan). Four years ago, the Fredericks, who are also active in rescue work, brought home a little Boston from the Delaware County SPCA, hoping to place her in a good home. Before long, the little dog captured their hearts and one year later she earned her CD, and a year to the day after that, she completed her CDX, placing her number-two in

Edwin Luther with Ch. Luther's Gallant Lord Bruce CDX, winning at the Wichita Kennel Club in 1949.

obedience in the US. Since then Molly has now reached the next level of obedience work and has the coveted title of Utility Dog after her name. This award is all the more sweet when accomplished with a rescue dog!

Edwin Luther, who was very active in showing his Bostons in conformation, owned and showed in the obedience ring Ch. Luther's Gallant Lord Bruce, CDX. Mr. Luther wrote that he showed this dog in 1949 and 1950 from the West Coast to the east of the Mississippi, and border to border, where he was the top scoring dog in most of the shows where he appeared. He wrote, "Bruce was an absolute joy to show, always eager to please and he loved the attention that the crowds gave him when and after he performed." Those who show dogs in both conformation and obedience know that when you have a dog who loves to be a ham, in addition to wanting to please, your job to reach first place becomes much easier to accomplish.

If you are so inclined, there is much that you can do with your Boston Terrier to keep you both busy! Obviously, any owner who can make these achievements in the obedience ring has love for the dog, training ability and bushels of patience! I had a friend who was active in obedience and she always said that her obedience dogs taught her humility.

Jypsies Jenn UDX, Can. CD, TD, owned by Gary and Susan Herber, going over the hurdle.

Scent discrimination by the very talented Jypsie.

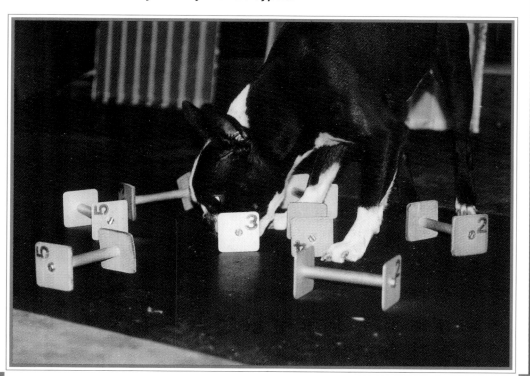

The see-saw event at an agility competition.

OTCH. Brother Mack Duff, owned by Ellen Dresselhuis, the first Obedience trial Champion in Boston Terrier history!

HIGHEST SCORING
DOG OBEDIENCE

CYCLONE COUNTRY
KENNEL CLUB

OCTOBER 1991

Meyer Photo
By SHARON

Holly, Jypsie and Jake, performing the down-stay.

AGILITY

Agility is a relatively new sport having come to the United States from England. The handler and the dog, working as a team, go through a timed obstacle course. Scoring is simple and objective, based upon the dog completing all of the obstacles and the speed with which this is accomplished.

In order to compete in this sport, you must belong to an all-breed club or an dog's height at the withers and never more than one-and-a-half times the height.

Bruce and Sandy Crook, of Brandy Bostons, wrote all of their dogs do agility, including Ch. Bo-K's Lillie Lee, their great grandmother who looks and acts like a puppy on course. Their Bostons' motto is "Get a life—go Agility!" They like agility as it is "play motivated, like taking the kids to the park—the

Ch. Brandy's Rowdy Kate NA, NAC, owned by Bruce and Sandy Crook.

obedience club where there are individuals who support this event. The obstacle course requires not only substantial space but the obstacles themselves are fairly large and extensive.

Basic obstacles are a see-saw, pipe tunnel, collapsed tunnel and weave poles. Jumps and hurdles will include the broad jump, tire jump and high jump. Jumps are at least one time's the ultimate sport for bonding!" Sandy and her dog Doc are full-time members of the SuperDogs National Performance Team. The SuperDogs is a family show and perform in a wide variety of venues around the world. As an aside, Sandy is the author of a book published by T.F.H. *Lop Rabbits As Pets.* A versatile lady herself, as well as having versatile Bostons!

Ch. Brandy's Doc Holliday over the 18-inch jump at a USDAA-sanctioned agility test. Owners, Bruce and Sandy Crook.

Many dog shows now hold agility as an exhibition. The ring can be easy to find as spectators can be four deep around the entire area. A great deal of enthusiasm emanates from all quarters: cheers from the spectators, barking from the dogs and loud encouragement from the handlers. This is a fun sport and not for the weak of heart!

Two other Boston owners who have done well in agility are Nancy Ames of Roseville, Minnesota, and Ann Croft of San Diego.

From the *AKC Gazette*, "The Boston can stand on two legs almost as easily and gracefully as on four, jumps with agility to truly surprising heights and can do a pirouette that would make a whirling dervish green with envy." And this was written in 1942, decades before the exhibitor was familiar with Agility trials!

Rocket Man competing at the Lickety Splits Flyball Tournament. He was the number-one Boston in North America in 1996.

The talented Brandy Bostons through the hoop!

Ch. Brandy's Rose of the Cimarron OA, OJC, OGC, EAC.

Ch. Brandy's Doc Holliday OA OJC, OGC, EAC, FDCh.

Am-Can. Ch. Anchor's Special Jazz CDX, Can. CD, practicing her agility work. Owner, Dot Truman.

Ch. Brandy's Doc Holliday OA OJC, OGC, EAC, FDCh., over the hurdles at a flyball competition.

Jonathan Milner taking Ch. Jondan's Legend by Crockett through the paces.

Ch. Brandy's Rose of the Cimarron OA OJC, OGC, EAC, making it look easy!

The family of Brandy Bostons: Bruce and Sandy Crook with agility winners, Ch. Brandy's Doc Holiday NA, Ch. Brandy's Rose of the Cimarron NA, Ch. Brandy's Little Britches, and Ch. Brandy's Rowdy Kate NA.

Epilogue

Considerable research went into the writing of this book and as the chapters grew in length, I became more aware of the tremendous amount of work that individuals have done, not only for this breed but for the sport of dogs in general. Without these individuals the world of dogs would not be the same.

The newcomer often does not realize what makes a breed, a breeder or a breed club. The breeders who were mentioned in this book did not "make it" in a year, two years or even five years. It took years of breeding to establish a line, and it took years of being a foot soldier to become well-known in the breed. Those who have made it and who have a kennel name that is recognized as producing winning dogs have been the individuals who have stuck with it through the lean years and the good years, through the years of some great winners and the years when the wins were not so great. Meanwhile, these individuals worked for the breed, belonged to their all-breed clubs, carried the coffee pots to the matches and stood all day in the rain to ring steward.

The true dog person is knowledgeable about other breeds and often judges matches for other breed clubs. The true fancier will give of his time, and often money, to the Boston Terrier Club of America, the national club, and to his local Boston Terrier club as well. He will serve on the committees, attend

Three champions out of the same litter: Ch. Al-Mar's Armed & Dangerous, Ch. Al-Mar's By Invitation Only and Ch. Al-Mar's Formal Attire, sired by Ch. Maestro's Special Whiz ROM out of Ch. Al-Mar's Irish Escapade ROM.

Ch. Bo-K's Ebony and Ivory, bred by Bob and Karen Milham and owned by Leana Terrill.

Champion littermates at one year old, Ch. Rees' Amber Elegance and Ch. Rees' Captivating Cameo, sired by Ch. Maestro's Billy Whiz Bang out of Ch. Bar None's Elegance, owned by Richard and Janet Rees.

meetings and do the grubby work that it sometimes seems that no one else wants to do. He will help new individuals with grooming and handling and he will be pleased when a Boston Terrier goes Best in Show, even if it isn't of his own breeding.

The old-timers of the breed, those who have been around for twenty, thirty and forty years, understand this. They have paid their dues and continue to pay them with few complaints. And this is what makes a great dog person.

Breed and show your dogs, but also get active in the purebred-dog community. Learn as much as you can about other breeds and the issues that affect all dog owners. You can't learn it in a day and you don't become a star in a year. But stay with it and you will gain knowledge, make friends and have enough good times for a lifetime.

And to close, Edwin Luther wrote, "I loved my Boston with all my heart. He loved me even more. Bostons do that, don't they?"

Snoozing in the sun, here's Jake at 14 weeks of age, owned by Ron and Sharon Berkland.

Betty Montgomery, spending time with her Am-Can. Ch. Krak-Mont Dejon by Balint.

Ch. ML's Karadin Robmar's Suede, owned by Marian Robben.

A winning team of Bostons: here's Cheri, Bizzie, Vickie and Dolly, owned by Leasa and Arnold Tyrrell of Knoty Bostons.

At ten months of age, Can. Ch. Kennedy's Storm Watch Bramley sees no clouds in his future! Bred by Vicki Kennedy and owned by Ann Lord.

International sensations and three high-C's, here's Jose Carreras, Luciano Pavarotti and Placido Domingo, bred by the Colquohouns of New Zealand.

JR's Kewpie Katrina by GiGi's, owned by Joan Webster. Sired by Ch. Rosedale Tuxedo Cowboy out of GiGi's Golden Girl.

Two top winners from S. Maxine Uzoff, Ch. Oui's Hi Stepn Coca Cola Cowboy CD, ROM and Ch. Lux's Scarlet O'Hara of Al-Mar.

Ch. Maximillian's Duchess Wine, a Top Ten Bitch, shown winning BOS at Westminster in 1991 under judge Betty Krause. Breeder, Barbara Bate. Handler, Ann McCammon. She is the dam of Ch. Maximillian's Mon Petit.

Ch. Maximillian's Mon Petit, winning BOS at the National Specialty Centennary show in 1991 under breeder-judge Blanche L. Smith. Breeder, Barbara Bate. Owners, Joanne Hearst and Ann McCammon.

Ch. O.J. First Class Fortune Cooky and her father Ch. Justamere's Showman Deja Vu both became top winners in the early 1990s—Group winners as well as BIS and specialty show winners. Deja Vu was the fourth all-time producing sire in the breed and the Top Boston in 1990. Owners, Joanne Hearst and Ann McCammon.

Index

Page numbers in **boldface** refer to illustrations. For the reader's convenience, all titles have been removed from dogs' names.